To my mother
Beulah Cain Haseltine

*East and
Southeast Asian
Material Culture
in North America*

Recent Titles in
Material Culture Directories

Irish American Material Culture: A Directory of Collections, Sites,
and Festivals in the United States and Canada
Susan K. Eleuterio-Comer, compiler

Hispanic-American Material Culture: A Directory of Collections, Sites,
Archives, and Festivals in the United States
Joe S. Graham, compiler

East and Southeast Asian Material Culture in North America

COLLECTIONS, HISTORICAL SITES, AND FESTIVALS

Compiled by
Patricia Haseltine

Material Culture Directories, Number 3
Margaret Hobbie, Series Editor

Greenwood Press
New York • Westport, Connecticut • London

Library of Congress Cataloging-in-Publication Data

Haseltine, Patricia.
   East and Southeast Asian material culture in North America :
collections, historical sites, and festivals / compiled by Patricia
Haseltine.
      p.   cm.—(Material culture directories, ISSN 0743-7528 ; no.
3)
   Bibliography: p.
   Includes indexes.
   ISBN 0-313-25343-9 (lib. bdg. : alk. paper)
   1. Asian Americans—Material culture—Directories.   2. Asians—
Canada—Material culture—Directories.   3. Historical museums—
United States—Directories.   4. Historic sites—United States—
Directories.   5. Festivals—United States—Directories.
   6. Historical museums—Canada—Directories.   7. Historic sites—
Canada—Directories.   8. Festivals—Canada—Directories.
   I. Title.   II. Series.
E184.06H37   1989
973'.0495'0025—dc20   89-2187

British Library Cataloguing in Publication Data is available.

Library of Congress Catalog Card Number: 89-2187
ISBN: 0-313-25343-9
ISSN: 0743-7528

First published in 1989

Greenwood Press, Inc.
88 Post Road West, Westport, Connecticut 06881

Printed in the United States of America

The paper used in this book complies with the
Permanent Paper Standard issued by the National
Information Standards Organization (Z39.48-1984).

10 9 8 7 6 5 4 3 2 1

Contents

Series Foreword

In the past twenty-five years, the United States and Canada have seen a great upsurge of interest in ethnicity. This interest was first fueled by the civil rights movement in the United States and the move toward multi-culturalism in Canada. It has been rekindled by the United States Bicentennial, the publication and broadcast of <u>Roots</u>, and the centennial of the Statue of Liberty. It has spawned journals and newsletters, national organizations, special libraries, and festivals. It has been equally popular with academics and the general public.

Interest in the study of material culture, as a means of explicating traditional and popular culture, has also grown steadily in recent years. Since 1980, journals and newsletters have been founded to disseminate ideas about material culture, studies, monographs and anthologies of major articles have been published, and museums large and small are taking a more careful, culturally based approach to the interpretation of their collections.

The Greenwood Press series of Material Culture Directories brings together the study of ethnicity and material culture. Modeled on Greenwood's <u>Museums</u>, <u>Sites</u>, <u>and</u> <u>Collections</u> <u>of</u> <u>Germanic</u> <u>Culture</u> <u>in</u> <u>North</u> <u>America</u> (compiled by Margaret Hobbie, 1980), the series is the first concerted effort to locate and describe ethnic material culture and photographic collections in the United States and Canada. Many directories in the series will go beyond the German volume by including chapters on festivals, which in some communities afford outsiders the best--often the sole--access to a group's material culture.

Each volume in itself raises fundamental questions about the role of material culture in ethnic identity--what has been preserved, by whom, where, and why? But the series is not meant to stand alone. It is, rather, an attempt to facilitate further studies on the role of material culture in the lives of North American ethnic communities--studies of the signs and symbols that help establish ethnic identity, or studies of "everyday" material culture and the extent to which it reflects traditional or mainstream values.

The compilers hope, as well, that the series will
encourage ethnic communities to begin to look at their past
in terms of their material culture. They hope that history
museums and other potential repositories will collaborate
with local ethnic communities in initiating or increasing
efforts to collect objects and photographs that reflect the
ethnic experience.

Patricia Haseltine's compilation of East and Southeast
Asian American collections, sites, and festivals includes
material from fourteen nations and many more ethnic groups,
thereby indicating the tremendous linguistic, racial, and
cultural diversity represented by the term "Asian." But
however diverse in origins, immigrants from Asia to North
America have shared a long history of economic struggle
marked by recurring prejudice. Only very recently have their
contributions to the cultures of the United States and Canada
been appreciated. Material culture collections offer new
insights into the lives of Asian immigrants to North America,
for whom written documentation is often sparse. This
directory thus opens important avenues to the examination and
recognition of the lives of Asian Americans and Asian
Canadians.

                                        Margaret Hobbie
                                        Series Editor

Preface

The study of Asian immmigration to the United States and
Canada is a relatively new interest emerging in the 1960's,
a century after the major emigrations from China and Japan
began.   Most Asian American studies research examines the
social history of various ethnic groups or their relationship
to other social groups.   Recognition of one's own roots,
accompanied by the struggle for equal opportunity, motivates
the research of many descendants of early Asian immigrants,
but, no matter what their origins, researchers in this field
value each Asian immigrant group for its contribution to the
variety and depth of culture in the United States and Canada.
Not only a social science, Asian American studies
depends upon historical research, and the recent oral
history emphasis has provided many good personal accounts
of immigration and settlement.   Personal experiences are also
reflected in prose and poetry, as well as in other arts.
This directory is primarily designed to promote the
study of Asian American and Asian Canadian history, folklore,
and art.   It assumes that repositories of material culture,
historical sites, and current festivals are important
resources for gaining an understanding of the cultures
represented.   Accurately reconstructing the lives and
experiences of our predecessors is difficult if not
impossible, but seeing what objects they used in their daily
lives, what they wore on festival and ordinary occasions, the
arts they produced, and the buildings they have constructed
puts us in closer touch with their values and aesthetics and
enriches our own.
Chapter 1 lists objects, as well as photographic and
historical records, maintained in museums and historical
societies in the United States and Canada.   An attempt has
been made to focus on objects presumably used by immigrants
or objects from the periods of early immigration; however,
the distinction between these materials and those collected
by travellers to Asia before or during these periods of
immigration has not always been possible.   Chapter 2 lists
sites bearing significance on the lives of Asian immigrants
and reflects not only their settlement primarily in Hawaii,

California, and British Columbia, but their diffusion and
concentration in various cities and geographical areas. Some
sites, those of detention or relocation, also draw attention
to the fact that Asian settlement in North America was
disrupted by periods of anti-Asian sentiment. In the case of
Japanese Americans, this disruption during World War II may
in part explain the dearth of settlement sites of Japanese
Americans in comparison to the preservation of sites of
Chinese American settlement. Chapter 3 focuses on the ways
artistic and material culture traditions are maintained in
current festivals.

The Asian traditions represented in this directory
include those of East and Southeast Asia. Ideally each
culture and nation should have a volume to itself. However,
as this work shows, most museums which accession materials
from one Asian ethnic group also hold materials from other
Asian immigrant cultures. The cultural groups most
extensively represented in all sections of this directory are
Chinese, Japanese, Filipino (or Pilipino), and Korean
peoples, groups whose migration across the Pacific began in
the middle and late 1800's. Although many of the objects of
Southeast Asian provenance in museums were collected by
travellers to Asia, more recent immigration from Vietnam,
Cambodia, and other Southeast Asian areas is also reflected
in some collections. What the directory has not been able to
show adequately is that each of these larger national groups
comprises different geographical or ethnic groups. For
example, immigrants from China may belong to different ethnic
groups or subcultures, and refugees from Vietnam may be of
Chinese origin. Refugees from Cambodia have different
cultural backgrounds, and immigrants from Indonesia belong to
different subcultures. However, when a museum or historical
agency has provided such information, the precise group
represented is indicated in the entry for that repository.

Acknowledgments

This directory project was begun and has proceeded under the gracious direction of Margaret Hobbie whose volume on German American material culture has provided the guidelines for my research. I am grateful for her patience and assistance.

I also wish to thank the curators of museums for providing detailed responses to the questionnaire and to several people who have been especially helpful: Debbie Kraybill and David DeVito of the Office of the National Register; Diane Rogers, Curator of the Port Moody Station Museum in Port Moody, British Columbia; Grace Rung-hua Chen, who conducted several personal interviews in New York City's Chinatown; Jean Thompson, for her assistance with Hmong materials in Merced, California, and Hsiao-mei Liu, Chiang Lu, and Lin Ching Yuan, who assisted me in the coverage of festivals and collections in California. In Hawaii, I would like to especially thank Christina R. N. Lothian of the Lyman House Memorial Museum, Rhoda Kamura of the Bishop Museum, and Barbara Hoogs of the Honolulu Academy of Arts, all of whom went out of their way to explain the sources of their collections to me. For their assistance with the text of the directory, I want to thank David Haseltine and Yang Hui-yun, as well as Greenwood Press editors Cynthia Harris and Christine S. Taylor. I am also very grateful to Sr. Eleanor Mary Buckley of Providence University in Taiwan for her support and encouragement which made it possible for me to continue and share my research.

My mother has provided the inspiration for my interest in material culture and folk art, and it is to her that I dedicate this text.

INTRODUCTION

History of East and Southeast Asian Immigration to North America

Immigration to the United States and Canada of people from Asia began in the first half of the nineteenth century with the arrival of a few seamen, craftsmen, domestics, students, and merchants. Gradually, as labor was needed on sugar plantations, in mining, and in railroad building, better trade and diplomatic relations were established one after the other with China, Japan, and Korea, and workers were sought in these countries and in the Philippines. Attempts to increase the labor force set the tone for large-scale immigration of Asians to North America.

United States-Chinese trade relations first linked the Eastern port cities of the United States with the southern Chinese province of Kuangtung, already thriving from its trade relations with other Western nations. The outcome of the Opium War which made Hong Kong a British state and opened up several free ports stimulated emigration from southern China in spite of an official Ching decree forbidding it. Periods of flood and drought, challenges to land ownership, and subsequent peasant revolts drove many peasants into the cities of the South to find employment, and, in the 1850's, it was from these cities, especially Canton, that thousands of young men were hired--some of them pressured or tricked into indenture--by the cooperation of Chinese and Western agents. On contract, laborers were shipped to Peru, Cuba, Mexico, Southeast Asia, Canada, Hawaii, and California. Others migrated on their own, paying for their passage by selling land or businesses.

Hawaii and California were the first disembarkation points for Chinese workers. While it was still a monarchy, remaining so until 1898, Hawaii became a stop for British and American ships in the China trade. Chinese who had abandoned ship from these trading vessels, in association with Anglo-American entrepreneurs, helped develop the sugar industry in Hawaii (Char and Char, 3-5). Although at first the labor of

native Hawaiians was used in the cane fields, other sources
of labor were needed as well, and soon the shipping of
plantation workers from China began. After five years, when
their labor contracts expired, most Chinese chose to
establish their own farms or businesses rather than continue
working in the cane fields. Family members would then join
them to build up businesses. In his youth, Dr. Sun Yat Sen,
who would later lead the revolution against the Ching
Dynasty, was sent to live in Hawaii where he spent six years
helping an elder brother who was a storekeeper and attended
an English language missionary school. Later it was from the
overseas Chinese in Hawaii, San Francisco, and New York that
Sun received support for the successful revolution of 1911.

Upon the discovery of gold in California in 1848,
Chinese hoping to improve the economic situation of their
families made the arduous journey from Kuangtung to the
"Golden Mountain." Between 1852 and 1854, more than 40,000
Chinese came to California to work in the mines. When the
mines were exhausted in the early 1860's, Chinese began to
settle in the San Joaquin and Sacramento Valleys of
California where they built levees and made swamp land
cultivatable. Others continued to work as cooks, launderers,
and provisioners, as they had in the mining towns, or opened
other shops. San Francisco's Chinatown became not only a
residential enclave for laborers returning from the mines,
but also a center of business and new employment. As
agriculture got underway in the valleys, these laborers who
resided in Chinatown formed a migratory labor force following
the harvest seasons of various crops (Nee and de Bary).
Mutual aid or benevolent associations with ties to important
families in Kuangtung, who first arranged passage for the
laborers, were also located in San Francisco. And when the
Central Pacific Railroad and, later, other railroad lines in
the West and Canada required construction labor for their
Western sections, the Six Companies, one such association,
arranged for the employment of many Chinese workers.

The early development of trade and labor between
companies in the United States and China preceded the
official recognition of these relations in the Burlingame
Treaty of 1862. The treaty required equal treatment of
Americans in China and Chinese in America, but in the post
Civil War depression, miners and other laborers, including
shoemakers and cigarmakers, began to feel threatened by the
Chinese who would work for low wages. As anti-Chinese
sentiment rose in California, various restrictions and taxes
began to appear with the purpose of driving out Chinese
laborers. Head taxes, for example, were levied on the
shipping companies, and special licenses were required for
foreign miners or later for those who hired foreign miners.
Even though bills passing the California legislature were
declared unconstitutional and in opposition to the intent of
the Burlingame Treaty, intensive lobbying and agitation,
along with personal violence against Chinese, culminated in a
revision of the Burlingame Treaty with China and finally the
Chinese Exclusion Act of 1882 (Sandmeyer). During the later
exclusionary period, Chinese who were still arriving on boats
to join family members already in the United States or to
fulfill labor contracts were interned on Angel Island in the
San Francisco Bay (see CA25 and CA105).

Exclusion of Chinese continued until the Act was repealed in 1943, largely as a result of pro-Chinese sentiment in the Second World War; only then did Chinese become eligible for citizenship. The 1952 Immigration and Nationality Act restricted immigration from Asia with a lower quota for that region than for the Western hemisphere, but the 1965 and 1976 ammendments have brought greater equality by setting a 20,000 limit per country and a system of preference categories. With the 1965 law favoring the immigration of educated professionals and relatives of Chinese Americans, Chinese more educated and affluent than the early laborers are now immigrating to the United States.

Similarly, in Canada the demand for great numbers of efficient laborers willing to work for low wages was curbed by prejudicial legislation against non-Europeans. Beginning in 1858, experienced Chinese laborers from the United States were hired to build the Canadian Pacific Railroad and by the 1860's the shipping industry began transporting workers from China. However, white workers organized protests and influenced government officials so that in 1885 the Chinese Immigration Act set a limit to the number of Chinese who could be transported on one ship and levied a head tax. In 1875, the Qualifications and Registration of Voters Act in British Columbia specifically denied the franchise to any Chinese. In 1900 and again in 1903, the head tax was raised, although exemption from the tax was made for established merchants and their families, diplomats, clergymen, tourists, students, and scientists. Later, the 1923 Immigration Act restricted new immigration, as well as the entry of dependents of citizens. Not until this act was repealed and the Citizenship Act of 1947 was passed were Chinese and other Asians given the franchise. Further legislation in 1962 and 1967 has, as in the United States, favored the immigration of the highly educated.

Emigration from Japan also began in the nineteenth century in spite of the shogun's decree against emigration on pain of death. In Hawaii in 1860, since neither the native Hawaiian population nor the Chinese laborers remained as workers on the sugar plantations, a special request was made by King Kamehameha IV of Hawaii to the shogun for a group of laborers to be sent to Hawaii to work on the sugar plantations.

Japanese migration to California began more slowly with some laborers going to the mainland when their contracts on the Hawaiian plantations had expired. One of the earliest attempts to establish an actual settlement of Japanese was that of John Henry Schnell. In 1869, Schnell tried to establish a silk colony in the foothills of the Sierra Nevada range west of Sacramento, but the farm failed, and the settlers dispersed (see CA112).

When the Chinese were driven out of mining communities and exclusion laws were hampering the needs of agriculture in California, Japanese began supplanting the Chinese in the growing fruit industries. At first, as with the early Chinese immigrants, single males made up the migrant labor force. Between 1910 and 1924, they travelled throughout the Sacramento, San Joaquin, and Santa Clara Valleys. Later, Japanese who had acquired families through the picture bride system or brought wives with them began to settle down in

farming communities, sharing equipment and labor with
families and friends from the same prefecture in Japan. As
Lukes and Okihiro note, Immigration Commission records for
1908 reveal that there was a cluster of five farming colonies
and 44 Japanese immigrant farmers who leased 273 acres in the
Santa Clara valley. These farmers grew mainly vegetables and
berries and worked in the local canneries (31, 63). In San
Jose, the Nihonmachi, or Japantown, served the religious,
medical, grocery, and service needs of surrounding Japanese
communities, and several boarding houses were maintained
where migratory workers lived in the off season (24-26). But
prejudices against Asians and exclusionary state laws against
land ownership, such as the Alien Land Law of 1913, increased
as people struggled with the poverty of the depression.
     In 1924, when the Chinese Exclusion Act was extended to
include all Asians, further immigration of Japanese was
greatly curtailed. In spite of the Gentlemen's Agreement by
which Japan would on its own accord limit emigration to the
United States, Japanese were no longer allowed to enter the
country. Unable to even apply for naturalization, some first
generation or Issei Japanese returned to Japan at this time;
others struggled with the laws, putting land in the names of
their children who as Nissei, second generation, could be
citizens, or cooperating with local white farmers in various
kinds of joint ownership.
     Japanese settlement in the United States faced an even
greater obstacle when the war with Japan began after the
bombing of Pearl Harbor. In February of 1942, by Executive
Order 9066, President Roosevelt declared that all peoples of
Japanese descent living in designated war zones along the
Pacific coast were to be evacuated and placed in inland camps
(see the following entries: AR104, CA118, CA122 and UT141).
Sixty-four percent of these people were already American
citizens, and many others of the first generation were people
who as Asians had been denied the right to naturalization
even though they had lived and worked in California most of
their adult lives. Farms were lost, and, although many
possessions were put in storage or left with friends, only a
small percentage of materials were actually recovered after
the release from the camps. In Hawaii, where Japanese made
up the majority of the work force and where less anti-
Japanese sentiment existed, only individuals actually thought
dangerous were taken to the internment site on Sand Island.
Some California families were given the choice of moving to
places in the central and eastern United States. In 1945,
when those put in camps were released, many found it
impossible to return to their former homes and occupations in
California (Weglyn). Some finally returned to vegetable and
berry farming in the central valley of California or opened
small businesses of their own in major cities, but the impact
of the World War II dislocation is still to be found. (A
similar policy of relocation was put into effect in Canada,
with Japanese families who had lived in British Columbia for
two generations being uprooted and moved inland.) The
poignant stories of Toshio Mori, first published in 1949,
illustrate the lives of Japanese Americans in California
during this troubled period.
     Replacing the Nihonmachi of the past are centers with
groceries, bookstores and restaurants, community centers with

entertainment, and homes for the elderly with ethnic foods and nurses who speak Japanese. In Los Angeles, the former Nihonmachi district which was in line for redevelopment was saved when the owners of small family-run businesses organized and collected funds to rebuild both from the city and local Japanese American organizations. By 1978, under architect-developer David Hyun, a modern district was built that in 1980 received a Federal Department of Housing and Urban Development Award and in 1985 the President's Federal Design Achievement Award.

Korean immigration to the United States in the period before the 1965 legislation which no longer restricted Asian immigration was limited to a few students and individuals supported by Christian missionaries to Korea. However, from 1903 to 1905, 7,200 Korean workers arrived in Hawaii on labor contracts. Through diplomatic and missionary channels, these men, women, and children were recruited to replace the diminishing numbers of Chinese and Japanese plantation workers. This source of labor was cut off when Korea became a protectorate of Japan in 1905 as a result of the Sino-Japanese War: then Japan did not allow any emigration of Koreans to the United States. Following the Second World War, Korean immigration once again could begin, subject to the limitations set on Asians by American immigration laws. Up until the 1965 legislation, the brides of American servicemen constituted the majority of Korean immigrants. Since then, however, yearly immigration has been over the 20,000 quota.

As in the beginning, various denominations of the Christian church continue to be an important link to the immigration of Koreans. A 1984 study by Won Moo Hurh and Kwang Chung Kim of the Koreans in Los Angeles, the city with the largest population of Koreans in the United States, shows that seventy percent of those participating in the study were Christian and that most of them belonged to Korean ethnic churches (158-159). Hurh and Kim characterize the adaption of Korean immigrants as "adhesive." That is, while on the one hand Koreans are Americanized, the new culture does not replace the previous one; instead, Korean traditional culture and social networks are maintained in addition to whatever traits of American culture immigrants acquire.

Filipinos (or Pilipinos) were, until Philippine independence in 1934, nationals of the United States. When Chinese and Japanese were being excluded, Filipinos were a remaining source of economical labor for the sugar and pineapple industries of Hawaii. Visayans, Tagalogs, and Ilocanos were at first recruited by the Hawaiian plantation owners, with the Ilocanos later becoming favored because they were already an agricultural people who sought relief from the impoverished barrios of Northern Luzon. Although many returned to the Philippines when their contracts expired, some settled in Hawaii and others came to the mainland United States. However, it was not until the immigration of Japanese had been sharply curtailed in 1908, that Filipinos took over a major part of the agricultural labor in California. Immigration increased in the years before 1930.

When the 1934 Tydings-McDuffie Independence Act, prompted by depression exclusionary sentiment as well as by the wishes of established Filipino American groups in the

United States, made the Philippines a nation, new immigrants
from the Philippines were no longer considered nationals;
they were now subject to the same restrictions as the other
Asian groups. However, during this period when a fifty
person quota restricted immigration, Hawaii was still allowed
exemptions to replenish its plantation work force, and in
California, the male population of Filipinos increased. The
Filipino migrant workers were then employed by the fruit and
vegetable growers in the valley districts to replace Chinese
and Japanese workers. Filipinos as yet could not become
citizens, however, and, as former nationals, some of them
wanted to serve in the armed forces, especially to defend the
Philippines against the invading Japanese. A special
dispensation was allowed them so that they could serve, and
later they were given the naturalization right. The classic
novel of Carlos Bulosan, <u>America</u> <u>Is</u> <u>in</u> <u>the</u> <u>Heart</u>, published
in 1946, gives a vivid insight into the lives of Filipino
immigrants to California who, while growing up as American
nationals, had to face the discrimination directed against
foreigners when they came to California as workers.

Indochinese immigrants, including peoples of Thailand,
Laos, Cambodia, and Vietnam, have also begun to find a place
for themselves in the United States and Canada. The Vietnam
War and other conflicts in Southeast Asia have made many
refugees seek homelands in other parts of Asia, in Europe, or
in North America. In the United States, special areas were
designated to receive the refugees and a sponsorship program
was instituted to help them find work and adapt to American
society. In 1983, 2300 Hmong women were engaged in various
sewing projects in fifteen states, and in Iowa, Washington,
and Minnesota, large-scale farming projects were begun (Fass
in Hendricks, et al, 202-206). However, the sewing and
farming projects were not lucrative enough to provide a good
livelihood, and many Hmong began opening cooperative grocery
stores. Since the original migration, many of these refugees
have relocated in places of their own choosing and are
attempting to continue their former lives as farmers or
fishermen. For example, Vietnamese have become fishermen in
Galveston, Texas, and in Monterery, California, while
Indochinese and Hmong in the San Joaquin Valley and in Fresno
and Orange County have taken up farming. Hmong and Mien
women, skilled at weaving, may provide a second income for
their families from the sale of their work. Some families,
many of whom are ethnically Chinese, have moved to major
cities, often in or near Chinatowns. In Honolulu, Houston,
Chicago and other cities, they have opened small businesses,
such as grocery stores and restaurants. In Chicago, the old
Chinatown on Argyle Street now contains a number of
Vietnamese small business concerns.

For East and Southeast Asians immigrating to North
America, the road to true settlement in a land promising
opportunity has been marked by hope, hardship, loneliness,
discrimination, and finally success. Traditional qualities
of great diligence, faithfulness to one's employer, and a
sense of humor made Asian immigrants a favored work force.
They engaged in construction projects that opened the West up
for further settlement and in farming endeavors that made the
land bear new fruit and vegetable varieties. They were
miners and fishermen, merchants, restauratuers, tailors, and

launderers. As writers they interpreted their experiences
for English readers. And as soldiers, they fought for their
adoptive countries. Ultimately, they were able to achieve
citizenship and franchise privileges in the lands they were
helping to build and defend. Recent immigrants, mostly
educated professionals, help the ethnic communities renew
their native sources of strength and further the artistic
achievements and the scientific and technological development
of America and Canada.

While offering their labor, skills, and arts, Asian
immigrants from China, Japan, Korea, the Philippines, Burma,
Cambodia, Malaysia, Indonesia, and Vietnam bring or make
articles of their material culture to use in their workplaces
and households, construct religious buildings for their
worship, and gather together on traditional festival
occasions to renew ethnic values still important to them in
their new lives. Retaining traditional arts and material
culture gives them and their children pride in their
heritages and allows them to make distinctive contributions
to the diversity and richness of American life. The
following directory, then, lists and honors their
contributions to the building of North America and hopes to
underscore their role as interpreters able to further greater
cooperation and trust between the nations of Asia and the
West.

References

Bulosan, Carlos. _America Is in the Heart: A Personal History_. Seattle: U of Washington P, 1973. (Reprint of New York: Harcourt, 1946.)

Char, Tin-Yuke, and Wai Jane Char, comp. and ed. _Chinese Historic Sites and Pioneer Families of the Island of Hawaii_. Honolulu: U of Hawaii P, 1983.

Con, Harry, Ronald J. Con, Graham Johnson, Edgar Wickberg, and William E. Willmott. _From China to Canada: A History of the Chinese Communities in Canada_. Toronto: McClelland & Stewart, 1982.

Fass, Simon M. "Economic Development and Employment Projects." In Hendricks, et. al., pp. 202-209.

Hendricks, Glenn L., Bruce T. Downing, and Amos S. Deinard. _The Hmong in Transition_. Staten Island, NY: Center for Immigration Studies, 1986.

Hurh, Won Moo, and Kwang Chung Kim. _Korean Immigrants in America: A Structural Analysis of Ethnic Confinement and Adhesive Adaptation_. Rutherford, NJ: Fairleigh Dickinson U P, 1984.

Lukes, Timothy J., and Gary Y. Okihiro. _Japanese Legacy: Farming and Community Life in California's Santa Clara Valley_. Cupertino, CA: California History Center, De Anza College. (_Local History Studies_, Vol. 31.)

Mark, Diane Mei Lin, and Ginger Chih. _A Place Called Chinese America_. Dubuque, IA: Kendall Hunt for The Organization of Chinese Americans, 1982.

Mori, Toshio. _Yokohama, California_. Seattle: U of Washington P, 1985. (Reprint of Caxton ID: Caxton Printers, 1949.)

Nee, Victor G., and Brett de Bary. _Longtime Californ': A Documentary Study of an American Chinatown_. Boston: Houghton, 1972.

Pido, Antonio J.A. _The Pilipinos in America: Macro/Micro Dimensions of Immigration and Integration_. Staten Island, NY: Center for Migration Studies, 1985.

Sandmeyer, Elmer Clarence. _The Anti-Chinese Movement in California_. Urbana: U of Illinois P, 1973.

Thernstorm, Stephan, ed. _Harvard Encyclopedia of American Ethnic Groups_. Cambridge, MA: Harvard UP, 1980.

Weglyn, Michi. _Years of Infamy: The Untold Story of America's Concentration Camps_. New York: Morrow, 1976.

East and
Southeast Asian
Material Culture
in North America

CHAPTER I

Collections

This chapter consists of descriptive entries of repositories of East and Southeast Asian material culture in the United States and Canada. The cultures of Chinese, Japanese, Korean, Philippine, Hmong, Indonesian, Malaysian, Thai, and Vietnamese immigrants are represented. The data were compiled from current editions of The Official Museum Directory, The Directory of Canadian Museums and Related Institutions, and The Directory of Historical Agencies in North America, other reference works listed in the bibliography, and from the responses to questionnaires mailed to over 200 potential repositories in 1986 and 1987.

Several types of repositories which maintain Asian American and Asian Canadian material culture are listed in this section: a.) anthropological or ethnographic museums which combine materials brought by immigrants with materials accessioned from the country of origin and materials donated by travelers to Asian countries; b.) immigrant historical societies and other historical societies which maintain records and materials brought or made by immigrant peoples; and c.) art museums which maintain some Asian material culture objects of high aesthetic value made in the country of origin or in the United States or Canada. With a focus on the period of immigration from the mid-1800's to the present, this listing excludes collections of ancient artifacts. It also excludes collections of fine art and collections of crafts made in famous craft centers almost solely for export.

The entries are arranged alphabetically by state or province, then by municipality, then by name of institution. Canadian entries follow United States entries. In each description the first mention of each Asian culture represented in that collection is capitalized.

In order to give an indication of the quantity of
materials available in a particular collection, the following
terminology is used: the word "a few" or no quantifier
indicates 1-5 items; the word "some" indicates 5-10 items;
"a number of" indicates 10-20 items; an exact number is given
for items numbering over 20 if this has been provided by a
curator; otherwise, a museum's holdings are designated as a
"major" or "large" collection.

AZ1   TOMBSTONE COURTHOUSE STATE HISTORIC PARK

Box 216
Tombstone, AZ 85638
(602) 457-3311

Hollis N. Cook, Park Manager
Staff: 4 permanent

The park maintains some objects representing the lives
of a colony of CHINESE miners who lived in Tombstone
in the late 1800's. These objects include clothing,
cooking utensils, a laundry iron, a tiger jug, an
abacus, and smoking apparatuses. Chinese traditional
graves in the town cemetery provide some information
concerning the lives of the Chinese population. The
park also has a number of black and white photographs
of Chinese cooks and miners.

Dates: late 1800's.

100% catalogued; 100% photographed.

Hours: daily 8-5. Admission fees: adults 1.00,
under 17 free.

Does not lend materials.

* * *

AR2   MILES MUSICAL MUSEUM

U.S. Highway 62 West
P.O. Box 488
Eureka Springs, AR 72632
(501) 253-8961

F.C. Miles and M.M. Miles, Founders
Staff: 4 permanent

The museum's John Yates Collection contains various
items of material culture, including CHINESE deities
and weapons, as well as jade and mahogany figurines,
jewelry, weapons, dancers' masks and coins from
Southeast Asia. Many of the items were collected by
Yates when he was a missionary in Java and Sumatra
from 1914 to 1924.

Dates: to early 1900's.

Hours: May 1-Nov. 1, daily 8:30-4:30. Admission
charge.

Does not lend materials.

* * *

CA3   LOWIE MUSEUM OF ANTHROPOLOGY

        Kroeber Hall
        Bancroft Way and College Ave.
        University of California, Berkeley
        Berkeley, CA 94720
        (415) 642-3681

        Frank A. Norick, Principal Museum Anthropologist

        Maintains ethnographic materials of Asian cultures
        and objects representing Asian American ethnic
        cultures. A major repository in California for such
        items.

        Presently computerizing materials.

        Hours: M-Tu, Th-F 10-4:30; Sat-Sun 12-4:30.
        Admission: $1.50.

                            * * *

CA4   MARSHALL GOLD DISCOVERY STATE HISTORIC PARK

        310 Back Street
        Coloma, CA 95613
        (916) 622-3470

        Staff: 9 permanent, 12 volunteer

        CHINESE articles are displayed in the park museum and
        in the Wah Hop and Man Lee stores on the site of James
        Marshall's 1848 gold discovery. Most of the items on
        display came from a Chinese store near Newcastle, CA
        removed for highway construction purposes. They
        include furniture, work tools, bottles, cups, bowls,
        plates, jars, teaware, and other eating and cooking
        utensils, including a soy bean grinder, straw apparel,
        everyday garments and shoes, porcelain pillow,
        decorative hangings, wooden chests, shop signs,
        smoking apparatuses, abacuses, coins, amulets, deities
        and bells. Also on display is a bowl from the nearby
        site of the JAPANESE Wakamatsu Tea and Silk Colony.

        Dates: 1800's and 1900's.

        80% catalogued; unknown no. photographed.

        Hours: daily 8 am to sunset. Admission: $2.00 per
        vehicle.

        Collection is available to researchers by appointment;
        items are rarely lent.

        Cf. WAKAMATSU TEA AND SILK FARM COLONY, CA112.

                            * * *

CA5   COLUMBIA STATE HISTORIC PARK

        P.O. Box 151
        Columbia, CA 95310
        (209) 532-4301

        Sherrin Grout, Ranger
        Staff: 13 permanent, 50 volunteer

        The collection contains CHINESE AMERICANA: baskets,
        bottles, jars, pots, cooking and eating utensils,
        decorative hangings, work tools, furniture, chests,
        wood and metal containers, shop signs, smoking
        apparatuses, ritual objects, part of a shrine, some
        calligraphy and painting, and many curing articles.
        Also has photographs of Chinese American subjects.

        Dates: specific dates unknown (mid 1900's).

        10% catalogued.

        Hours: W-Sun. No admission fee.

        Researchers can use collection by appointment.

                            * * *

CA6   DEL NORTE COUNTY HISTORICAL SOCIETY

        577 H Street
        Crescent City, CA 95531
        (707) 464-3922 or 487-6372

        Mary Lee Miller, Treasurer
        Staff: 13 volunteer

        In 1885, because of their unpopularity, the CHINESE
        who had worked on railroad construction, in the lumber
        mills and the canneries, and as domestic servants were
        driven out of Del Norte County and Humboldt City. To
        represent the period of Chinese residence in the
        area, the historical society maintains a collection
        of black and white photographs, mostly of miners, and
        a collection of newspaper articles from the Crescent
        City Courier concerning the history of Chinese in the
        county. The society also possesses a large collection
        of kitchenware, bambooware, and clothing, as well as
        pharmaceutical, ceremonial and recreational items
        collected throughout Northern California by Mrs. C.
        Madeline Wagner of Crescent City.

        Dates: 1849 Gold Rush Era to later settlement.

        Presently cataloging materials.

        Hours: May-Sept, daily 10-4. Fees: admission $1.50;
        research $5.00.

                                            California

CA6   (Del Norte County Historical Society)
cont.
        Does not lend materials; copies available for 10
        cents. Publication: <u>Chinatown Quest</u>: <u>The Life-
        Adventures of Dondina Cameron</u>, 1931.

                              * * *

CA7   FRESNO CITY AND COUNTY HISTORICAL SOCIETY

        7160 W. Kearney Boulevard
        Fresno, CA 93706
        (209) 441-0862

        Collection includes black and white photographs and
        documents of CHINESE and JAPANESE immigrants, as well
        as black and white slides of Chinese subjects.
        Artifacts include a Chinese drugstore and a Chinese
        Joss house altar.

        Dates: late nineteenth century.

        Hours: T-F 9-5. No fees.

        Does not lend materials.

                              * * *

CA8   SAN JOAQUIN COUNTY HISTORICAL MUSEUM

        Micke Grove Park
        P.O. Box 21
        Lodi, CA 95241
        (209) 368-9154

        Staff: 7 permanent, approx. 50 volunteer

        Located in the fertile central valley of California,
        this agricultural and historical museum illustrates
        the theme of "Man and the Soil" with artifacts from
        the pioneer settlement of Stockton, CA., beginning in
        1847 with a purchase of Mexican-owned land by Charles
        M. Weber, a farming and mining entrepreneur. In the
        1860's as the CHINESE left the gold mines, many used
        the agricultural knowledge and experience they had
        gained in the Pearl River basin of China to help
        reclaim over a quarter of a million acres of land in
        the northern San Joaquin and Sacramento Valley by
        constructing levees, ditches and dikes. They and
        other Asian farmworkers have since helped develop the
        agriculture of the area. Chinese articles in the
        museum's collection include a small number of cups
        and bowls, jars, cooking and eating utensils, everyday
        clothing, decorative hangings, farm implements,
        smoking apparatuses, a household shrine and festival
        lanterns. A number of embroidered theatrical

                                                    California

CA8   (San Joaquin County Historical Museum)
cont.

costumes, mandarin robes and other clothing, gifts to
the museum from Helen and Esther Cone and Joseph C.
Tope, represent the festival and ceremonial life of
the immigrants. The museum also has some JAPANESE
items: cups and bowls, ceremonial garments, dolls,
toys and fans.

Dates: primarily mid-nineteenth century.

100% catalogued. Library.

Hours: W-Sun 1-5. Park gate fee: $2.00.

Lends materials from the collection. Library use
by appointment. Publication: Toni L. di Franco,
Chinese Clothing and Theatrical Costumes in the
San Joaquin County Historical Museum.

* * *

CA9   CALIFORNIA HISTORICAL SOCIETY, HISTORY CENTER

6300 Wilshire Blvd.
Los Angeles, CA 90048-5247
(213) 651-5655

Janet Evander, Curator of the History Center

Maintains a collection of 150 black and white
photographs of CHINESE subjects dating from 1898-1940.

Hours: M-Th 2-6. No fees for research in center.

Does not lend materials, but photographic
reproductions can be purchased.

* * *

CA10 CRAFT AND FOLK ART MUSEUM

5814 Wilshire Blvd.
Los Angeles, CA 90036
(213) 937-5544

Contact Registrar or Librarian
Staff: 14 permanent

This international folk craft and art museum has a 200
item collection of JAPANESE toys, as well as a number
of Japanese masks, baskets, bedding pieces, everyday
and ceremonial garments, decorative hangings, and
cooking and eating utensils. Other Asian materials
held by the museum include CHINESE masks and
theatrical costumes, KOREAN masks and straw apparel,
INDONESIAN masks and batiks, and PHILIPPINE baskets.

California

CA10   (Craft and Folk Art Museum)
cont.
         Dates: mid 19th and 20th centuries.

         25% catalogued. Library.

         Hours: T-Sun 11-5. Admission fees: adults $1.50,
         children and seniors $.75.

         Lends materials from the collection only. Library and
         collection may be used by researchers.

                                  * * *

CA11   LOS ANGELES COUNTY MUSEUM OF ART

         5905 Wilshire Blvd.
         Los Angeles, CA 90036
         (213) 937-4250

         Dale Gluckman, Asst. Curator, Costumes and Textiles
         Staff: entire museum, 150 permanent; over 100
         volunteer

         The museum has a significant collection of textiles
         and costumes which includes CHINESE and JAPANESE
         bedding, everyday and ceremonial garments, decorative
         hangings, theatrical costumes, and jewelry, KOREAN
         everyday and ceremonial garments, PHILIPPINE everyday
         garments, THAI garments and jewelry, INDONESIAN
         garments and decorative hangings, as well as CAMBODIAN
         and LAOTIAN everyday garments. Textiles plans a
         special exhibition of Japanese Edo period kimonos for
         1991. The museum's holdings also include ceramics and
         wood carvings from many East and Southeast Asian
         cultures. A pavilion for Japanese art has recently
         been opened.

         Dates for textile collection: 19th and 20th c. and
         perhaps some 18th c.

         30% catalogued; 20% photographed. Relevant libraries
         include The Art Research Library and the Doris Stein
         Research and Design Center for Costumes and Textiles.

         Hours: T-Fri. 10-5; Sat-Sun 10-6. Admission fees
         vary.

         Does not lend materials. Libraries and textile
         collection may be used by researchers by appointment.
         Publications: Mary Hung Kahlenberg, Textile Traditions
         of Indonesia, 1977.

                                  * * *

                                                     California

CA12   COURTHOUSE MUSEUM, MERCED COUNTY HISTORICAL SOCIETY

21st. and N Streets
Merced, CA 95340
(209) 385-7426, 723-2401

Catherine Julien, Museum Technician
Staff: 1 1/2 permanent; 85 volunteer

The museum's chief Asian American holdings consist of
shrine furniture from a CHINESE shrine located in
Merced in the late 19th Century (probably 1875-
1880's), including an altar, altar pieces, deities,
carvings, a gong, and divining objects. Other Chinese
articles in the museum's possession are an association
sign, musical instruments, abacuses, ceramics, a
lottery basket and a 19th century domino game. The
society also maintains a small number of photographs
of Chinese American subjects. Recent museum
acquistions include HMONG pa ndao embroideries made
in Merced in 1986. Hmong refugees settling in Merced
are continuing native traditions of embroidery and
are preserving woven tapestries made in refugee camps
in Thailand which tell the story of their recent
emigration from Laos.

Dates: 1875-present.

No admission fee.

Does not lend materials. Collection can be used by
researchers by appointment.

* * *

CA13   CITY OF OROVILLE CHINESE TEMPLE

1500 Broderick St.
Oroville, CA 95965
(916) 533-1646

Jim P. Carpenter, Director of Parks and Trees
Staff: 9, plus 2 caretakers

Artifacts used by immigrant CHINESE families and other
Chinese of the same era are maintained in an 1863
temple complex maintained by the City of Oroville. The
folklife materials include a number of baskets, straw
sandals and other straw apparel, work tools, a gold
scale, printing materials and record books, a
cloissoné-making set, ceramic jars, pots, cups, bowls,
plates, teaware, vases and figurines, teakwood
miniatures, jewelry, 49 bronze mirrors, candelabra,
medicines and herbs, furniture and carved door panels,
bridal chair, chests, sweetmeat boxes, inkstones,
soapstone pieces, incense containers, cooking and
eating utensils, smoking apparatuses, a number of

CA13   (City of Oroville Chinese Temple)
cont.
        dolls and toys, 5 cases of shadow puppets, a set of
        child's dishes, fans, musical instruments, everyday
        and ceremonial clothing, a brocaded box, an
        embroidered purse, bedding, 29 decorative hangings and
        other tapestries, including an imperial pillar rug.
        Religious objects include amulets, altars and altar
        sets, deities with sedan carriers, door guards, parade
        drums, 30 festival poles, over 25 divining sticks,
        family shrines, parade shrines, incense, 100 pieces of
        fortune paper and temple money, parasols, masks,
        calligraphy, paintings, lanterns, grave stones and a
        large wood and gold leaf carving of the "Ship of
        Life." On special display is a 36 piece collection of
        men's, women's and children's clothing and accessories
        covering the period from 1850 to 1950.

        Dates: 1856-1900's.

        100% catalogued; 100% video-taped. Library.

        Hours: M-Tu, F-Sun 10-4:30; W, Th 1-4:30. Admission
        $1.50.

        Lends materials. Both the collection and the library
        may be used by researchers by appointment.

        Cf. OROVILLE CHINESE TEMPLE, CA123.

                              * * *

CA14   PACIFIC ASIA MUSEUM

        46 N. Los Robles Ave.
        Pasadena, CA 91101
        (818) 449-2742

        Deborah Bailey, Registrar
        Staff: 16 permanent, 150 volunteer

        Asian objects are housed in a CHINESE Imperial Palace
        style building and courtyard garden. In 1924, Grace
        Nicholson, an Asian art collector and dealer had the
        building constructed by Marston, Van Pelt and Maybury.
        Although the museum galleries have revolving
        exhibitions, the museum has many objects of Asian
        material culture. Chinese materials include some
        basketry, 184 ceramic pieces, 513 textiles, 87 pieces
        of metalwork, 52 pieces of furniture, screens and
        scrolls, 87 dolls and toys, 26 puppets, 181 pieces of
        folk art, sculpture and 139 utilitarian items.
        JAPANESE materials include baskets, 140 pieces of
        ceramic, 226 textiles, 76 metalwork pieces, some
        furniture, screens, 90 dolls and toys, 1010 prints,
        scrolls, 124 netsuki, and 34 pieces of jewelry.
        KOREAN objects include some basketry, a number of

CA14   (Pacific Asia Museum)
cont.

KOREAN objects include some basketry, a number of
ceramic pieces, 38 textiles, some metalwork,
furniture, a few utilitarian pieces, a few dolls and
toys, paintings and jewelry. PHILIPPINE materials
include some basketry, a number of ceramic pieces,
69 textiles, some metalwork, furniture, 24 utilitarian
objects, 42 weapons, jewelry, a few dolls and toys and
a painting. INDONESIAN materials include basketry, 64
textiles, metalwork, furniture, some jewelry, 25
utilitarian objects, a number of weapons, dolls and
toys, a number of paintings, a number of masks, and
sculpture. Other Southeast Asian cultures are also
represented by the museum's holdings.

Dates: 18th-20th c.

100% catalogued; 5-10% photographed. Library.

Hours: W-Sun 12-5. Admission: $2.00 adults.

Lends objects. Library and collection may be used by
researchers by appointment. Conducts explanatory
tours of garden and sponsors lectures, classes, art
auctions, art tours to Asia and festival celebrations.

* * *

CA15   CALIFORNIA STATE LIBRARY, CALIFORNIA SECTION

914 Capitol Mall
Mail: P.O. Box 942837
Sacramento, CA 94237-0001
(916) 445-4149

Richard Terry, Senior Librarian
Staff: 11 permanent

The California Section holds over 300 black and white
photographs of CHINESE subjects covering the years
1849 to the present and approx. 80 of JAPANESE
subjects covering the years from 1880 to the present.
Library has over 350 books on Chinese and 325 on
Japanese American history and culture. The California
Information File, unique to the California Section,
contains approx. 800,000 cards with more than 1
million citations. In this file are approx. 1900
cards referring to book, periodical, newspaper,
manuscript and biographical sources on Americans of
Chinese and Japanese, as well as KOREAN, PHILIPPINE,
and VIETNAMESE descent.

Dates: 1840's to present.

100% catalogued.

CA15   (California State Library, California Section)
cont.
        Hours: M-F 8-5. No fees.

        No appointment necessary. Many items may be
        photocopied or photographed. Research assistance
        is available for a fee. Some books, periodicals and
        microfilmed newspapers are available through Inter-
        Library Loan. Publication: New Arrivals in
        Californiana, a quarterly list of acquisitions.

                              * * *

CA16   CROCKER ART MUSEUM

        216 O Street
        Sacramento, CA 95814
        (916) 449-5423

        Paulette Hennum, Registrar
        Staff: 26 permanent, several hundred volunteer

        Museum has Asian and Asian American objects of
        material culture. It also displays a collection
        of 30 paintings by California natives, immigrants
        and visitors under the title "California, the Land
        and the People."

        Dates of California paintings: 1850-1930.

        Hours: Tu 1-9; W-Sun 10-5. Admission fees: $2.00 for
        adults.

        Lends collection items to other museums only; does not
        lend library books. Both collection and library can
        be used by researchers on site.

                              * * *

CA17   MINGEI INTERNATIONAL MUSEUM OF WORLD FOLK ART

        4405 La Jolla Village Drive 1-7
        San Diego, CA
        Mailing: P.O. Box 553
        La Jolla, CA 92038
        (619) 453-5300

        Tony Raczka, Registrar
        Leslie Bouffard, Assistant to the Director
        Staff: 6 permanent, approx. 75 volunteer

        Small gallery with revolving exhibitions. The museum
        holds an extensive collection of Asian and Asian
        American material culture. CHINESE objects include
        basketware, straw clothing, rattan furniture, ceramic
        cups and bowls, teaware, bronze spoons, everyday and
        ceremonial garments, decorative hangings, shoes,

                                              California

CA17   (Mingei International Museum of World Folk Art)
cont.

a wig case, dolls and toys, fans, kites, puppets, woodblock prints, a collection of 100 papercuts and a tomb rubbing. JAPANESE articles include baskets, straw clothing, ceramicware, iron kettles, lacquerware, work tools, everyday garments, pouches, jewelry, tapestries and wrapping cloths, chests, a sliding screen, umbrellas, a large number of dolls and toys, fans, kites, origami, woodblock prints, ritual objects, shrines, votive paintings, calligraphy, masks, as well as photographs. KOREAN materials include ceramicware, work tools, and woodblock prints. PHILIPPINE materials include baskets, straw clothing work tools, dolls, toys, and jewelry. Other possessions of the museum include VIETNAMESE musical instruments and clothing, as well as THAI ceramics, kites, puppets, a musical instrument, a coat of arms and weapons.

Dates: primarily 19th and 20th centuries.

100% catalogued; 50% photographed. Library.

Hours: T-Th 11-5; F 11-9; Sat 11-5; Sun 2-5.
Fees by donation.

Members can use library and collection. Lends materials. Catalogues available of Rites of Passage: Textiles from the Indonesian Archipelago, 1979 and Keisuke Serizawa: A Living Treasure of Japan, 1979.

* * *

CA18   CALIFORNIA HISTORICAL SOCIETY LIBRARY

2099 Pacific Avenue
San Francisco, CA 94109-2235
(415) 567-1848

Judith Sheldon, Principal Reference Librarian
Staff: 6 permanent, 8 volunteer

Library maintains photographs, manuscripts, pamphlets, books, posters, brochures, advertising cards and miscellaneous clippings. The black and white photographs include 46 folders on CHINESE, 18 folders on JAPANESE, 1 folder on KOREAN, and 2 folders on PHILIPPINE immigrant subjects. The book and pamphlet library contains approx. 200 Chinese, 130 Japanese, a number of Philippine and some Korean and VIETNAMESE immigrant materials. The collection also contains an oral history audio tape on Japanese American life.

Dates: mid-19th c. to present.

CA18   (California Historical Society Library)
cont.
         Hours: W-Sat 1-5. Fees: $3.00 per day for non
         members; $1.00 per day for students.

         No appointment necessary for research use. Collection
         is not loaned; no ILL. Publishes California History,
         a quarterly magazine, and The Courier, a bimonthly
         newsletter.

                              * * *

CA19   CHINESE CULTURE CENTER

         750 Kearny Street
         San Francisco, CA 94108
         (415) 986-1822

         Lucy Lim, Executive Director, Curator
         Staff: 9

         Sponsored by the CHINESE Culture Foundation of San
         Francisco, the center helps "promote and preserve the
         Chinese cultural heritage" and "provides a forum for
         the creative expression of Chinese and Chinese
         American artists of talent." Special community
         programs of the foundation include the annual Chinese
         Spring Festival brush painting classes, arts and
         crafts workshops and demonstrations, heritage and
         culinary walks in San Francisco's Chinatown and
         workshops in the martial arts, as well as in
         traditional music and opera. Exhibitions of art and
         photography with a wide range from ancient artifacts
         to modern Chinese art and Chinese American history and
         art are held year round in the center's gallery. The
         center also hosts live performances, film showings,
         and lectures by Chinese Americans and other guests.

         Gallery Hours: T-Sun 10-5. Admission is free.
         Heritage Walk fee: $9.00 adult; $2.00 children.
         Heritage Culinary Walk/Luncheon: $18.00 adult;
         $9.00 children.

         The Chinese Heritage Walk starts at the center and
         includes visits to the Chinese Historical Society of
         America, a Chinese temple, an herb store, churches,
         schools, community organizations and other points of
         interest. The Culinary Walk/Luncheon includes visits
         to noodle, sausage and fortune cookie factories, herb
         and tea shops, and grocery stores and ends with a "dim
         sum" luncheon. Tours are by reservation only and on
         weekdays only for groups of 6 or more.

         Cf. CHINESE HISTORICAL SOCIETY OF AMERICA, CA20.
         CHINESE NEW YEAR, CA149.

                              * * *

CA20   CHINESE HISTORICAL SOCIETY OF AMERICA

        17 Adler Place (Off 1140 Grant Ave.)
        San Francisco, CA 94133
        (415) 391-1188

        Ted Wong, President
        Staff: 1/2 permanent, 24 plus volunteer

        The historical society possesses a large collection of
        CHINESE immigrant artifacts and a collection of black
        and white photographs, documents and oral history
        tapes. On display in the small museum, which presents
        interpretive commentary on the experiences of Chinese
        in America, are an 1880 Chinese Buddhist altar,
        clothing and slippers of the 19th century, photos of
        Chinese working on the Central Pacific Railroad, a
        completely hand-made wheelbarrow, herbs and herb
        scales, gold scales, pipes, a fighting spear used in a
        local "tong" war, and a 14-foot California redwood
        sampan for fishing activities. Other artifacts
        maintained by the society include baskets, furniture,
        work tools, ceramicware, everyday garments, cloth
        altar pieces, flags, decorative hangings, abacuses,
        chests used on steamers coming from China, wood and
        metal containers, shop signs, dolls and toys, fans,
        puppets, musical instruments, deities, ritual objects,
        festival calligraphy and painting, as well as
        lanterns.

        Dates: 1850's to present

        Library.

        Hours: T-Sat. 1-5. No fees.

        Generally does not lend materials, but collection may
        be used by reseachers on the site. Sponsors a Chinese
        Heritage Walk conducted by docents from the Chinese
        Culture Center.

        Cf. CHINESE CULTURE CENTER, CA19.

                            * * *

CA21   NATIONAL MARITIME MUSEUM

        Fort Mason, Building 201 (at foot of Polk St.)
        San Francisco CA 94123
        (415) 556-3002

        Glennie Wall, Maritime Unit Manager
        Staff: 29 permanent

        Showing the history of water transportation from the
        1800's to the present, this museum has a collection of
        approximately 250 photographs of CHINESE subjects,

                                                    California

CA21   (National Maritime Museum)
cont.
        about 100 photographs of JAPANESE subjects and 50 of
        PHILIPPINE subjects. Also in the museum's possession
        are a Chinese geomancer's compass which still works,
        a navigation compass from Kowloon in a varnished
        wooden box, two drawings in a naive style, one of
        an unidentified Chinese warship and one of a junk or
        barge, a Japanese porcelain rice bowl, and five
        paintings of Philippine natives harvesting abaca
        fibers for rope making.

        Dates: late 19th and 20th centuries.

        100% catalogued; 75% photographed. Library.

        Hours: June 1-Aug. 31, daily 10-6; rest of year 10-5.
        No fees for museum.

        Does not lend. Library and collection can be used by
        researchers. No appointment necessary.

                              * * *

CA22   CHINESE HISTORICAL SOCIETY OF SOUTHERN CALIFORNIA
        ARCHIVES

        Chinese Historical Society
        1514 Princeton Street
        Santa Monica, CA 90404
        (213) 828-6911

        S. Kwok, Archivist
        Staff: 6-10 volunteer

        The historical society maintains numerous materials
        on CHINESE American subjects. Major collections
        include the Southern California Chinese American Oral
        History Collection of photos, documents and
        transcripts of oral history tapes, and the Robert A.
        Nash collection of materials on Chinese junks on the
        Pacific Coast and fishing villages. Archives has 1500
        black and white and 200 color photographs, 100 black
        and white and 100 color slides, 400 audio tapes with
        161 summaries, as well as numerous historical
        documents.

        Dates: 19th c. to present

        10-20% catalogued. Library.

        Hours: by appointment. Fees: by schedule.

        Does not lend materials, but sells copies. An
        appointment is needed for use by researchers.
        Publishes the biannual Gum Saan Journal which focuses
        on Chinese American history in Southern California and

                                              California

CA22   (Chinese Historical Society of Southern California
cont.   Archives)

        the Southwest. Has published <u>Linking</u> <u>Our</u> <u>Lives</u>, a
        book on the history of Chinese American women in
        Southern California.

                              * * *

CA23   STANFORD UNIVERSITY MUSEUM OF ART

        Stanford University
        Stanford, CA 94305

        Patrick J. Maveety, Curator of Asian Art
        Staff:13 permanent; 3 volunteer; 75 docents

        Folk or ethnic arts constitute about 10% of the
        museum's Asian collection. These include the
        following CHINESE materials: some teaware, 50-60
        ceremonial garments and cloth pieces, a number of
        decorative hangings, a theatrical costume, furniture,
        a chest, screens, a number of smoking apparatuses,
        a jade piece, a number of fans, and 50 papercuts.
        JAPANESE materials include a number of baskets,
        40 articles of teaware, 25 ceremonial garments or
        cloths, smoking apparatuses, and 35-40 dolls and
        toys. KOREAN materials held by the museum include
        some ceremonial garments and cloth, as well as
        cooking and eating utensils. INDONESIAN items
        include 50 ceremonial garments or cloths and masks.

        Dates: 19th and 20th centuries.

        50% of folklife collection photographed, not
        catalogued. Personal library.

        Hours: Tu-F 10-5; Sat-Sun 1-5. No fees.

        Will lend materials. Collection and personal library
        available to researchers.

                              * * *

CA24   THE HAGGIN MUSEUM

        1201 N. Pershing Avenue
        Stockton, CA 95203-1699

        Joanne Avant, Registrar
        Staff: 10 permanent

        About 5% of the museum collection contains ethnic and
        folk materials. The "Storefronts Gallery" displays a
        CHINESE herb shop brought almost in toto from
        Stockton's Chinatown when the area was redeveloped.
        The shop is arranged as it was when used, the drawers

                                              California

CA24   (The Haggin Museum)
cont.

and bins filled with herbs and potions. Other Chinese
objects held by the museum include ceramicware, an
abacus, chests, lacquerware containers, and musical
instruments. JAPANESE materials include ceramic
pieces, laquerware containers, 50 woodblock prints,
and weapons. The museum also possesses KOREAN
ceramics and smoking apparatuses, as well as
PHILIPPINE weapons.

Dates: c. 1900 to 1950.

50% catalogued; 50% photographed. Library has local
history materials, but does not specialize in Asian
American materials.

Hours: Tu-Sun 1:30-5.

                              * * *

CA25   ANGEL ISLAND STATE PARK AND ANGEL ISLAND ASSOCIATION

P.O. Box 318
Tiburon, CA 94920
(415) 435-5537

Catherine (Cassie) Burke, State Park Ranger
Staff: 1 permanent, 10 volunteer

On this island in the San Francisco Bay CHINESE
immigrants were detained in barracks. The Chinese
Exclusion Act of 1882 and subsquent legislation
required intensive interrogation for family members of
Chinese Americans. While they were awaiting
questioning and making appeals, detainees wrote or
carved poems expressing their despair on the barracks'
walls. Some representative articles on display in the
barracks museum include herb and pill bottles, a cloth
bundle containing herbs, an opium pipe, hand-made
fishing hooks, a brass lock, a metal button, a ball-
sock, a gai moh yin which is similar to a shuttle cock
but made of paper and cardboard, and a carved stick,
either for a stick game or used as a spool for yarn.
The park also has 100 lantern slides of Chinese,
JAPANESE, and KOREAN subjects dating from the 1910's
to the 1920's, as well as 50 black and white prints of
buildings, staff and immigrants. Is currently adding
several interpretive exhibits. Other articles from
the island's collection are maintained at the Office
of Interpretative Services, 1280 Terminal, West
Sacramento, CA 95691.

Dates: 1910-1940.

50% catalogued; 50% photographed. Informal Library.

CA25   (Angel Island State Park and Angel Island Association)
cont.
          Hours: mid-Feb-Oct, holidays and weekends 11-4. Also
          open upon request. Park can be reached by commercial
          ferry service from Tiburon or San Francisco daily June
          to early Sept and weekends and holidays Sept-May.
          (For current schedules call Angel Island State Park
          Ferry Co., Tiburon, 415-435-2131 or Harbor Carriers,
          Inc. of San Francisco.) Admission is free to museum.

          Materials from library and collection are not loaned,
          but copy machine is available. (Donations accepted for
          use.) Publication: H. Mark Lai, Judy Yung and Genny
          Lim, Island, 1980 (contains poems from barracks'
          walls, oral histories and narrative history).

          Cf. ANGEL ISLAND DETENTION CENTER, CA105.

                              * * *

CA26   TRINITY COUNTY HISTORICAL SOCIETY MUSEUM

          P.O. Box 333
          Weaverville, CA 96063
          (916) 623-5211

          Karen Engelhart-Brown, Curator
          Staff: 10 plus volunteer

          The museum has a collection of material culture, of
          which 80% is folk or ethnic. The CHINESE folklife
          collection includes some of each of the following:
          ceramics, ceremonial garments and cloth, abacuses,
          cooking and eating utensils, containers, furniture,
          smoking apparatuses, weapons, fans, and medicine
          bottles. The society also possesses a number of
          photographs and immigrant documents.

          Dates: 1850's-1880's.

          100% catalogued; 1% photographed.

          Hours: Winter, Tu 10-5. No fees at present.

          Does not lend materials. Collection is available to
          researchers by appointment.

                              * * *

CA27   WEAVERVILLE JOSS HOUSE STATE HISTORICAL PARK

          P.O. Box 1217
          Weaverville, CA 96093
          (916) 623-5284

          Contact Unit Ranger
          Staff: 1

                                                    California

CA27   (Weaverville Joss House State Historical Park)
cont.

The collection maintained in the CHINESE village-style
temple complex focuses upon the story of the Chinese
gold miners who settled in the Weaverville area.
Materials located in the priest's quarters include
some early immigration period clothing, furniture,
mining tools, bottles, jars and pots for general food
storage and cooking, other household items, sleeping
mats, everyday garments, some processional and
association banners, an imperial umbrella, cloth
signs, chests for everyday use, a theatrical costume
from Hunan and abacuses. In the temple are found
eight deities with six attendants, a few brass cymbols
and hand gongs, a drum, a fan, a few paintings
reversed on glass, and a few lanterns. A few
photographs of some Chinese oldtimers and of the Joss
House over the years are also held.

Dates: approx. 1874-1925.

100% will be catalogued; 100% photographed for park
records. Library.

Does not lend materials, but both collection and
library can be used on site.

* * *

CO28   WESTERN HISTORICAL COLLECTIONS, UNIVERSITY OF
COLORADO

Norlin Library
Campus Box 184
Boulder, CO 80309
(303) 492-7242

Cassandra M. Volpe, Library Technician
Dr. John A. Brennan, Curator
Staff: 3 permanent

The Western Historical Collection of the University of
Colorado Library maintains materials on CHINESE,
JAPANESE and PHILIPPINE subjects. These include black
and white stills and documents of Chinese, Japanese
and Philippine ethnic groups, as well as Japanese
American oral history tapes.

Dates: primarily mid to late 19th century.

85% catalogued. Main library holds books on Asian
American subjects.

Hours: M-F 10-5. No fees.

Does not lend materials.

* * *

CO29   DENVER PUBLIC LIBRARY, WESTERN HISTORY DEPARTMENT

1357 Broadway
Denver, CO 80203-2165
(303) 571-2009

Eleanor M. Gehres, Manager

The Western History Department has 33 black and white
photos of CHINESE and 7 photos of JAPANESE immigrant
subjects, as well as an extensive collection of books
on both ethnic groups. The library also has
documents on Chinese subjects and a good file of 26
photographs on the Japanese American Relocation Center
at Amache, Colorado in the 1940's. Extensive indexing
is provided for newspaper and magazine articles from
1865 covering Asian Americans in Denver, in Colorado
in general and in the West. Asian Americans also
appear in additional photographs which are filed under
subjects other than ethnic group.

Dates: mid-late 19th c. and early 20th c.

Hours: M-W 10-9; Th-Sat 10-5:30; Sun 1-5. No fees.

Does not lend materials, but photocopies allowed.
Use of some materials (MSS and rare) may require an
appointment.

* * *

CT30   THE SLATER MEMORIAL MUSEUM

The Norwich Free Academy
108 Crescent
Norwich, CT 06360
(203) 887-2505, ext. 218

Joseph P. Gualtieri, Director
Staff: 4 permanent

Approximately 10% of the museum's East and Southeast
Asian holdings are folk or ethnic material culture.
CHINESE materials include a quantity of ceramicware, a
quantity of ceremonial garments, many decorative
hangings and shoes, a few chests, many pieces of
furniture, many dolls and toys, many fans, a few
paintings, and a few dieties and tomb figures.
JAPANESE items include a large quantity of ceramics,
a quantity of ceremonial garments, many decorative
hangings, theatrical costumes and shoes, a few chests,
many pieces of furniture, a few screens, a quantity of
netsuke pieces, many sword and sword guards, many wood
carvings, many dolls and toys, a few fans, a quantity
of origami and stencils, a quantity of woodblock
prints, and a few paintings, deities, ritual objects,
and shrines. KOREAN materials include a few ceramic

CT30   (The Slater Memorial Museum)
cont.
         figures and a quantity of ceremonial garments. The
         museum also has JAVANESE materials--a quantity of
         batiks, a few dolls and toys and many puppets--and
         SIAMESE deities.

         Dates: 17th-20th c.

         100% catalogued. A small research library.

         Hours: Sep-June, weekdays 9-4, Sat and Sun 1-4;
         Summer, daily 1-4. Closed Mon and holidays. No
         admission fees.

         Does not lend materials. Collection and library may
         be used by researchers by appointment.

                               * * *

DC31   NATIONAL ARCHIVES, MOTION PICTURE BRANCH

         NNSM-2W, Research Rm. G-13
         8th and Pennsylvania Ave., NW
         Washington, DC 20408
         (202) 786-0041

         NNSM Archivist

         The archives maintains newsreel footage concerning the
         life of JAPANESE Americans and first generation
         Japanese immigrants who were removed by the War
         Relocation Authority from the West Coast and relocated
         in concentration camps inland. Other films show the
         training and record of Nisei soldiers in WW II. Also
         available are 28 radio broadcasts containing reports
         on Nisei soldiers and speeches on WRA activites by
         Dillon S. Meyer, the director of the Authority.

         Dates: 1942-1943.

         Hours: M-F 8:45-5:15.

         Does not lend materials; appointment necessary for
         viewing films; no appointment necessary for use of
         card catalog. The archives also sells copies of
         films, video tapes, and sound recordings.

                               * * *

DC32   SMITHSONIAN INSTITUTION

         National Museum of American History
         Division of Community Life, Rm 4100
         Smithsonian Institution
         Washington, DC 20560
         (202) 357-2385

                                    Connecticut-District of Columbia

DC32   (Smithsonian Institution)
cont.

       Richard E. Ahlborn, Curator
       Staff: 4 permanent, 3 volunteers in division

       75% of the East and Southeast Asian holdings in the
museum are ethnic American material culture. CHINESE
immigrant materials include ceramics, everyday
garments, papercuts, shop signs, work tools, masks,
abacuses, and furniture, including tables, a stool,
a mat and an apothecary cabinet, as well as approx.
20 photographs. Laotian KMHMU items include some work
tools, musical instruments, a model house and
protective religious objects. JAPANESE ethnic history
in the United States is interpreted in a special
exhibition entitled "A More Perfect Union: Japanese
Americans and the United States Constitution."
Assembled by the Division of Armed Forces History,
this exhibition will be on display until Oct. of 1992.
Many items, including furniture and other objects
associated with the internment camp experience, as
well as objects associated with the World War II 442
Regiment of Japanese Americans, will remain in the
Division of Community Life collection when the
exhibition closes.

       Dates: 1890-1980.

       100% catalogued; 1% photographed.

       Hours: 10-5. No admission fees.

       Lends to museums. Collection may be used by
researchers by appointment.

       Cf. COOPER-HEWITT MUSEUM, Smithsonian's National
         Museum of Design, NY 63.

* * *

DC33   THE TEXTILE MUSEUM

       2320 S. Street NW
       Washington, DC 20008
       (202) 667-0441

       Curator, Eastern Hemisphere
       Staff: 25 permanent, 120 volunteer

       The textile museum has a significant collection of
150-200 INDONESIAN cermonial garments and cloth with
furnishings for ceremonial hanging. It also maintains
CHINESE textiles, including 20-30 ceremonial garments,
a number of furnishings for ceremonial hanging, and
some decorative hangings, 20-30 JAPANESE ceremonial
garments and some everyday garments, some PHILIPPINE

DC33   (The Textile Museum)
cont.
        everyday garments, some Upland VIETNAMESE JARAI
        everyday garments and a number of THAI ceremonial
        garments.

        Dates: 19th and 20th c.

        98% catalogued; 10% photographed. Library.

        Hours: 9-5. No fees, but donations requested.

        Conditional lending policy. Collection and library
        may be used by researchers.

                            * * *

FL34   MORIKAMI MUSEUM OF JAPANESE CULTURE

        4000 Morikami Park Rd.
        Delray Beach, FL 33445
        (305) 495-0233

        Larry Rosensweig, Director
        Staff: 8 permanent, 85 volunteer

        Located at the site of a former colony of JAPANESE
        immigrants which flourished from 1910-1925, a museum
        constructed in 1976 now holds a large collection of
        400 dolls and toys and a number of straw items,
        including farm tools, various containers and a Meiji
        period mail carrier's rain cape. Other materials in
        the museum include ceramics, a few everyday and
        ceremonial garments, cooking and eating utensils, wood
        or metal containers and work tools, smoking
        apparatuses, kites, and musical instruments.
        Religious articles include shrines, a deity, lanterns,
        and 40 minga (votive paintings and prints).

        Dates: Late 19th-present.

        5% photographed. Library.

        Lends materials from collection to qualified
        institutions. Library materials are loaned to
        members and teachers. Researchers may use collection
        and library by appointment.

                            * * *

HI35   LYMAN HOUSE MEMORIAL MUSEUM

        276 Haili Street
        Hilo, Hawaii, HI 96720
        (808) 935-5021

HI35   (Lyman House Memorial Museum)
cont.
         Leon Bruno, Director
         Brian Tanimoto, Curator
         Christina R. N. Lothian, Archivist-Librarian
         Staff: 7 full time and 6 part time permanent, 35
         volunteer

         Adjacent to the home built by David and Sarah Lyman,
         missionaires to Hawaii in the 1830's, is a museum
         with ethnic exhibits. Several Asian peoples settled
         on the island of Hawaii and in the town of Hilo when
         their plantation work contracts expired. The museum
         gives a chronology of the successive periods of
         settlement and provides artifacts to represent each
         group. The JAPANESE materials on display include
         several pieces of work clothing, wedding garments, and
         documents pertaining to immigrant labor. The CHINESE
         display has ceramic pieces, clothing and a restored
         shrine, which was originally dismantled and brought
         from Kuangtung, then reassembled for a temple in Hilo.
         Although a tidal wave destroyed the temple, the shrine
         from it was preserved by the Wang family and donated
         to the museum. Chinese herbs used in the work camps
         and a grinding wheel are also found in this section.
         KOREAN costumes, as well as PHILIPPINE baskets and bed
         coverings are also on display. A special exhibits
         gallery displays items of regional interest. In one
         such exhibit, a complete Japanese hospital has been
         reassembled. (In Hawaii from 1907-1960, 11 ethnic
         hospitals run by Japanese doctors served the health
         needs of the immigrant workers.) The museum archives
         maintains an extensive library of books, 10,599
         photos, prints and rare newspapers.

         Dates: 19th and 20th c.

         Hours: M-Sat 9-4. Fees: adults $2.50; children $1.25.

         Library available to researchers.

                          * * *

HI36   BERNICE PAUAHI BISHOP MUSEUM
         HAWAII IMMIGRANT HERITAGE PRESERVATION CENTER

         1525 Bernice Street
         P.O. Box 19000-A
         Honolulu, Oahu, HI 96817
         (808) 847-3511, ext. 171

         Rhoda Kamura, Curator-Immigrant Heritage Center
         Museum staff: 100 full time, 200 part time, 49
         volunteer

         A natural history museum and center for Pacific-
         wide ethnological research, the Bishop Museum has

HI36   (Bernice Pauahi Bishop Museum
          Hawaii Immigrant Heritage Preservation Center)
cont.

          permanent displays, as well as special exhibits
          interpreting the heritage of immigrant ethnic groups.
          Displays in the main museum hall include items
          representing several Asian American cultures. CHINESE
          materials include musical instruments, furnishings
          from several temples once located in Honolulu and in
          Kapaia, clothing and accessories, peasantware, cooking
          and eating utensils, and business orders and
          documents. The JAPANESE materials include armaments,
          ceramic decanters, masks, baskets, carpenter tools,
          wooden tobacco pouches, and kimonos. Other objects
          displayed include KOREAN ceramics and passport
          pictures, OKINAWAN kimonos, and FILIPINO baskets, rice
          farming implements, textiles, ornaments, and betel and
          lime containers. The Hawaii Immigrant Heritage
          Preservation Center houses special exhibits which
          relate history from the viewpoint of the common man,
          collecting, documenting and preserving not only items
          brought by the immigrants from their separate
          cultures, but also objects they made of local Hawaiian
          materials and objects they shared with each other in
          Hawaii. These items, in addition to various documents
          maintained by the center number in the thousands.
          Among these are the artifact collection donated by the
          Hawaii Chinese History Center and donations from
          Japanese and Filipino ethnic associations. Also
          maintained by the center are over a thousand
          photographs in albums donated by immigrant families.

          Dates: 1889 to pre-World War II.

          100% catalogued and indexed. Library and photo
          archives.

          Hours: Museum, daily 9-5. Immigrant Heritage Center,
          M-F 1-4; special visits may be arranged by
          appointment.

          Lends for exhibition. Materials are available to
          researchers. Access to collection in storage by
          appointment. The Bishop Museum Press's Dept. of
          Anthropology publishes books, monographs and research
          reports on the cultures of Hawaii and the Pacific.

                              * * *

HI37   HAWAII CHINESE HISTORY CENTER

          111 N. King St., Room 410
          Honolulu, Oahu, HI 96817
          (808) 521-5948

          Contact Executive Director
          Staff: 12 volunteer

HI37   (Hawaii Chinese History Center)
cont.
        The Hawaii Chinese History Center maintains a large
        collection of material relating specifically to
        CHINESE immigrants and their families. This important
        collection includes 800 photographs, black and white
        as well as color, 1,800 slides, 110 oral history
        tapes, 1,100 books (more in Chinese than English), and
        a 26 linear foot vertical file of clippings in English
        and Chinese. The Center currently directs and assists
        in historical and geneological research projects.

        Dates: mid-1800's-present.

        Hours: M, Th, F 10-12 noon. No fees. Library.

        Does not lend materials. Collection can be used by
        researchers by appointment only. The Center publishes
        a quarterly newsletter and, in collaboration with the
        University of Hawaii Press, publishes one or two books
        a year on the Chinese in Hawaii, such as Violet Lai's
        He Was a Ram, 1965.

                            * * *

HI38   HAWAII STATE ARCHIVES

        Iolani Palace Grounds
        Honolulu, Oahu, HI 96813
        (808) 548-7460

        Susa Shaner, Photo Archivist

        The State Archives maintains black and white
        photographs and documents of CHINESE, JAPANESE,
        KOREAN, and PHILIPPINE subjects in Hawaii. Many
        show the life and work on the sugar plantations of
        these early emigrants from Asian countries, while
        others provide illustrations of the growth of urban
        areas.

        Dates: 1850's to present.

        100% catalogued.

        Hours: 8-4:15. No fees.

        Does not lend materials. No appointment necessary for
        use by researchers.

                            * * *

HI39   HAWAIIAN HISTORICAL SOCIETY

        560 Kawaiahao Street
        Honolulu, Oahu, HI 96813
        (808) 537-6271

                                              Hawaii

HI39   (Hawaiian Historical Society)
cont.
        Barbara E. Dunn, Librarian and Executive Secretary
        Staff: 1 1/4 permanent, 1 part-time volunteer

        The society has an extensive collection of materials
        on the Hawaiian Islands in general, including 33
        black and white photographs of JAPANESE, 15
        photographs of CHINESE and a few photographs on KOREAN
        and PHILIPPINE immigrant subjects. The library
        contains books relating to all of these immigrant
        cultures.

        Dates: 1950's.

        Catalogued.

        Does not lend materials; collection can be used by
        researchers. The society publishes The Hawaiian
        Journal of History. Past issues include articles
        about Chinese, Japanese and Koreans in Hawaii.

                                * * *

HI40   HONOLULU ACADEMY OF ARTS, LENDING COLLECTION

        900 South Beretania Street
        Honolulu, Oahu, HI 96814
        (808) 538-3693, ext. 56.

        Barbara Hoogs, Keeper
        Staff: several permanent, several volunteer

        While Asian fine arts and ancient artifacts are on
        display in the main part of the museum, objects of
        material culture and folk arts comprise a lending
        collection for educational use by the general public.
        This collection of arts and crafts was obtained from
        the families of Asian immigrants and from travellers
        to Asia from Hawaii. CHINESE objects include roof
        tiles, a number of baskets, writing materials,
        candlesticks incense bowls and burners, coins and
        paper temple money, a large collection of clothing and
        accessories, including brocade jackets, coats and
        robes, theatrical costumes, scarves, silk and bamboo
        hats, leggings, shoes and jewelry, textiles and
        textile craft design samples, a number of dolls,
        several sandalwood fans, flags, numerous pieces of
        teakwood furniture, door panels, household objects,
        musical instruments, including a peddler's rattle, a
        processional drum, cymbals, a gong, a ti-chin
        (a Chinese fiddle) and a bamboo flute, ceramic, stone
        and wood sculpture, miniature funeral and wedding
        procession figures, models of junks, a ricksha and
        cart with horse. Mounted prints illustrating Chinese
        artifacts, architecture and customs are also
        available. On reserve is a significant collection of

HI40   (Honolulu Academy of Arts)
cont.

embroidered needlework and an extensive collection of
hand and shadow puppets. JAPANESE articles include
architectural models and ornaments, armament
accessories, stick reed mats, bamboo baskets and flat
reed trays, book arts, including books on brush
drawing, ricepaper music books, children's books,
writing implements, and scrolls, various toys, Boys'
Day dolls and accessories, a large collection of
Girls' Day dolls and accessories, screens and bowls,
other festival objects, such as Bon Dance scarves,
shrines, prayer beads, incense burners and votive
panels, a stone figure of Jizu--patron of children,
tea ceremony objects, peasant clothing and priest's
robes, theatrical costumes, men and women's <u>kimonos</u>,
numerous costume accessories including fans, hair
ornaments, handbags, hats, <u>obis</u>, parasols, shashes,
and scarves, craft implements and materials, household
objects--ceramic peasantware, lacquer boxes, trays,
and bowls--, numerous masks, puppets, and a large
collection of cotton, linen, satin and silk textiles.
Mounted prints of Japanese architecture, sculpture,
prints, paintings, customs, and gardening can also be
borrowed. KOREAN materials include architectural
models, baskets, a temple bell, everyday and
ceremonial clothing and accessories, coins and
currency, dolls, household items, musical instuments,
and embroidered and appliqued pillows. Various
articles representing PHILIPPINE, INDONESIAN, and
VIETNAMESE cultures are also maintained in the lending
collection.

100% catalogued. Library.

Hours: Tu-F 1-4; Sat 8-noon. No admission charge or
lending collection fees.

Loans articles mainly to schools, libraries and
other public institutions. Borrowing privileges are
also extended to grade school, high school and
university students with the permission of a teacher,
and to others for educational purposes.

Cf. BON ODORI AND FLOATING LANTERN FESTIVAL, HI160
    BOYS' DAY, HI161.
    GIRLS' DAY, HI164.

* * *

HI41   UNIVERSITY OF HAWAII-MANOA, CENTER FOR ORAL HISTORY

Social Science Research Institute
Porteus Hall 724
2424 Maile Way
Honolulu, Oahu, HI 96822
(808) 948-6259

HI41   (University of Hawaii-Manoa, Center for Oral History)
cont.
        Warren S. Nishimoto, Director
        Staff: 4 permanent

        Established by the Hawaii State Legislature in 1976,
        the center records and preserves oral history
        interviews with all of the peoples of Hawaii. The
        oral history center has 30 tapes on CHINESE, 100 on
        JAPANESE, 2 on KOREAN, and 100 on PHILIPPINE
        immigrants. The tapes relate to such subjects as
        sugar and coffee plantation work, the 1924 Filipino
        Strike on Kauai, Japanese Issei history, the OKINAWAN
        experience in Hawaii and women in the pineapple
        canneries. Video tapes, slide shows and publications,
        which are mainly multi-ethnic in scope, are produced
        on these and various other themes of the islands'
        history. The collection also has photo displays on
        all of the oral history projects, on the oral history
        process, on mochi (rice cake) pounding and on Buddhism
        in Hawaii. The center disseminates transcripts to
        libraries, researchers, students and the general
        community and trains groups and individuals interested
        in oral history research.

        Dates: late 19th c. to present.

        100% catalogued.

        Hours: see University of Hawaii schedule.

        Lends materials. Transcripts are also available at
        State Regional Libraries, the University of Hawaii
        system libraries, and the Hawaii State Archives
        Collection. Video tapes and slide shows are available
        at university libraries.

                              * * *

HI42   KAUAI MUSEUM

        P.O. Box 248
        Lihue, Kauai, HI 96766
        (808) 245-6931

        Kenneth A. Kapp, Acting Director
        Staff: 6 permanent, 18 volunteer

        About 20% of the museum's holdings are Asian ethnic
        materials. Many of the JAPANESE items, which are the
        most numerous, reflect the history of sugar plantation
        workers brought to Kauai to work on the Grove Farm and
        other sugar cane plantations on this island.
        Traditional Japanese culture is extensively
        represented by the following items: baskets, a large
        collection of ceramics, including jars, pots, plates,
        cups, teaware and various decorative articles,

                                                    Hawaii

HI42   (Kauai Museum)
cont.

textiles and costumes, including 35 everyday garments
and some ceremonial garments and decorative hangings,
25 housekeeping implements, cooking utensils, screens,
smoking apparatuses, dolls and toys, 30 fans, musical
objects, masks, chests and furniture. CHINESE
material culture is represented by numerous ceramic
pieces, some everyday and ceremonial garments,
decorative hangings, chests and furniture. The KOREAN
materials include a few ceramic pieces and some
ceremonial garments. PHILIPPINE basketware is also
found in the museum.

Dates: 1850's to early 1900's.

96% catalogued; 5% photographed. Library.

Hours: M-F 9:30-4:30. Admission: $3.00.

Occasionally lends items for study and special
exhibits.

Cf. GROVE FARM, HI134.

* * *

ID43   IDAHO STATE HISTORICAL SOCIETY

610 Julia Davis Dr.
Boise, ID 83702
(208) 334-2120

Jody Hawley, Registrar
Staff: 40 permanent

Asian immigrant folk culture and history are
represented by the collections of the Idaho State
Historical Society. The CHINESE materials include
baskets, a large collection of ceramic jars, pots
teaware and spoons, 25 everyday garments, some
ceremonial garments and decorative hangings, a money
counter, 300 coins, wood and metal cooking and eating
utensils and containers, screens, shop signs, smoking
apparatuses, work tools and scales, dolls and toys, a
number of musical instruments, a number of shrines,
deities, ritual and divining objects, festival
calligraphy and painting, a number of lanterns, and an
extensive collection of herbs and medicines that
belonged to Dr. C. K. Fong and his son, Dr. Gerald Ah
Fong who practiced traditional Chinese medicine in
Boise, Idaho from 1890-1960. The museum also has some
JAPANESE ceramic pieces, straw apparel, wood and
metalwork containers, and a doll. The PHILIPPINE
materials include straw apparel and a number of
armaments. The society also has photographs of

ID43   (Idaho State Historical Society)
cont.
        materials include straw apparel and a number of
        armaments. The society also has photographs of
        several immigrant groups: 100 photographs of Chinese
        subjects, 150 of Japanese subjects and 10 of
        VIETNAMESE subjects.

        Dates: 1860-present.

        75% catalogued; 3% photographed. Library.

        Hours: M-Sat 9-5; Sun 1-5. No admission fee.

        Has discretionary lending policy. Library and
        collection are accessible to researchers only by
        appointment. Access to the Fong collection is very
        limited. Exhibit in place is "Journey to the Gold
        Mountain: The Chinese in Idaho." Relevant
        publication: Idaho Yesterdays, Winter 1958-59 issue.

                              * * *

ID44   UNIVERSITY OF IDAHO ASIAN COMPARATIVE COLLECTION

        Alfred W. Bowers Laboratory of Anthropology
        University of Idaho
        Moscow, ID 83843
        (208) 885-7075 or 6123

        Priscilla Wegars, Research Associate and Curator

        The laboratory collects examples and photographs of
        "representative objects of Asian manufacture" found in
        "archaeological contexts in North America." Artifacts
        represented in the collection include over 150 CHINESE
        food and beverage containers and table ceramics, opium
        smoking paraphernalia, 20 medicine bottles, gambling-
        related items, a basket, a deity, product labels and
        miscellaneous hardware and implements. Also has a
        number of JAPANESE ceramics and medicine bottles and
        an extensive collection of slides illustrating Asian
        sites and artifacts, including 1000 Chinese, 100
        Japanese and a few PHILIPPINE subjects.

        Dates: 1850-1987.

        100% catalogued; 5% photographed. Library.

        Hours: by appointment.

        Lends materials. Emphasizes site and artifact
        identification and documentation. Publishes
        a quarterly newsletter. Two bibliographies, and one
        dissertation are available for purchase. Research
        assistance also available.

                              * * *
                                                        Idaho

IL45   SOUTHERN ILLINOIS UNIVERSITY MUSEUM

Southern Illinois University
Carbondale, IL 62901
(618) 453-5388

Lorilee Huffman, Museum Registrar
Staff: 8 permanent, 25 volunteer

Significant in the museum's Southeast Asian holdings
is an extensive collection of VIETNAMESE material
culture including a large collection of baskets, work
tools, fans, ceramics, a large collection of
ceremonial garments, cooking and eating utensils,
smoking apparatuses, and lanterns. Also has
25-50 films on Vietnamese culture. CHINESE ceramics,
a JAPANESE musical instrument, KOREAN woodblock
prints, and PHILIPPINE masks are also held.

Dates: 1960-1970.

100% catalogued; 1% photographed. Small library.

Hours: M-F 9-3; Sun 1:30-4:30. No admission fee.

Occasionally lends materials. The collection and
library can be used by researchers by appointment.

* * *

IN46   INDIANA UNIVERSITY FOLKLORE ARCHIVES
        ARCHIVES OF TRADITIONAL MUSIC

Folklore Archives and Archives of Traditional Music
103 Morrison Hall
Bloomington, IN 47401
(812) 335-3652

Staff: 3 part-time assistants in Folklore Archives
       1 permanent and several part-time assistants in
       Archives of Traditional Music

The archives has transcribed material available on
Asian and Asian American material culture traditions.
CHINESE subjects cover customs and religion and
include material collected in New York City's
Chinatown on the Moon Cake and material on funeral and
marriage ceremonies collected in Detroit and Chicago
Chinatowns from the Michigan State Collection. The
archives also has a collection of anecdotes, ethnic
jokes and sayings told by non-Chinese about Chinese.
JAPANESE subjects cover traditional wedding customs,
festivals and Japanese American foodways and include a
a first person account of the Bon Dance as observed in
Hawaii by Luana Fukutome. PHILIPPINE subjects include
material on traditional musical instruments, folk
dances and folk plays as recorded by Joy Viernes

IN46   (Indiana University Folklore Archives and
cont.   Archives of Traditional Music)

Enriquez, as well as transcripts on festivals and
custom. Transcripts on MALAY and THAI customs and
festivals are also maintained, including a description
of the Songkran Festival. The Archives of Traditional
Music maintains recordings of folk music from many
Asian countries, including the Richard Waterman
recordings of Chinese folksongs and traditional music
made in Chicago in 1946 by a visiting Peking Opera
Company and a collection of recordings of festival
street music in Chicago's Chinatown.

Dates: 1940's to present.

Folklore Book Collection in Main Library.

Hours: M-F 9-5 and by appointment. No fees.

Does not lend materials, but copies of some materials
available to researchers.

Cf. BON DANCE, HI159.
                                    * * *

IN47   INDIANAPOLIS MUSEUM OF ART

1200 W. 38th St.
Indianapolis, IN 46208
(317) 923-1331

Peggy S. Gilfoy, Curator-Textiles and Ethnographic Art
Staff in dept.: 1 permanent; 5 volunteer (in museum:
125 permanent; over 200 volunteer)

The museum has a large collection of East and
Southeast Asian textiles and costumes. The CHINESE
materials include 200 ceremonial garments and cloth,
50-100 decorative hangings and a few theatrical
costumes. JAPANESE textiles include 50-100 ceremonial
garments, a number of decorative hangings and a few
theatrical costumes. PHILIPPINE materials include
25-50 ceremonial garments and a few decorative
hangings. INDONESIAN materials include 100-150
festival garments and cloth and a few decorative
hangings.

Dates: 18-20th centuries.

98% catalogued; 5% photographed. Library.

Hours: Tu-Sun 11-5. No admission fees.

Does not lend materials. Collection and library may
be used by researchers by appointment.

                          * * *
                                            Indiana

IN48   THE SHELDON SWOPE ART GALLERY

      25 South Seventh Street
      Terre Haute, IN 47807-3692
      (812) 238-1676

      Janet Ballweg, Registrar
      Staff: 8 permanent, no. of volunteer staff varies

      Approximately 50% of the gallery's permanent East and
      Southeast Asian holdings are of material culture.
      CHINESE items include ceramics, some everyday
      garments, a belt hook, everyday chests, containers,
      furniture, screens, a plaque, woodblock prints, wall
      panels, carvings, religious objects, masks, and animal
      figures. JAPANESE objects include straw umbrellas,
      a large collection of teaware and other ceramics,
      everyday garments, _obi_ buckles, clogs, an everyday
      chest, furniture, a screen, a panel, a scroll, a doll,
      ornaments, ritual objects, masks and a collection of
      53 woodblock prints. Also in the museum's possession
      are KOREAN straw and cloth slippers, a PHILIPPINE
      table cover and wooden mule figure, and SIAMESE
      puppets and an amulet.

      Dates: 17th-19th centuries.

      100% catalogued; 10% photographed. Library.

      Hours: Tu-F 10-5; Sat-Sun 12-5. No admission fee.

      Materials are loaned with approval of museum director.
      Collection and library can be used by researchers by
      appointment, but the library has only a few Asian
      materials.

* * *

IA49   PUTNAM MUSEUM

      1717 West 12th St.
      Davenport, IA 52804
      (319) 324-1933

      Janice Hall, Curator of Anthropology
      Staff: 7 permanent, 20 volunteer

      80% of the museum's collection of East and Southeast
      Asian materials is of folk or ethnic origin. The
      CHINESE materials include straw apparel, a number of
      ceramic pieces, 56 everyday garments, some ceremonial
      garments, some decorative hangings, wood and metal
      cooking and eating utensils, containers, a number of
      pieces of jewelry, furniture, abacuses, smoking
      apparatuses, work tools, a number of weapons, dolls
      and toys, some fans, a number of puppets, some musical
      instruments, papercuts, shrines, 64 deities, amulets,

IA49   (Putnam Museum)
cont.
         a number of ritual and divining objects, 34 pieces of
         festival calligraphy and painting, lanterns and a
         bride's chair. JAPANESE materials include a number of
         baskets and bamboo or straw apparel, ceramics,
         especially teaware and vases, a 107 piece collection
         of everyday garments, a few ceremonial garments, some
         decorative hangings, chests, 55 cooking and eating
         utensils, 37 containers, a number of pieces of
         furniture, jewelry, smoking apparatuses, work tools,
         100 weapons, 76 dolls and toys, a number of fans, some
         kites, 20 musical instruments, some papercuts, 145
         woodblock prints, 32 shrines, 50 deities and other
         religious objects, a number of pieces of festival
         calligraphy and painting, some lanterns, 29 masks, and
         a Jinriksha. KOREAN materials include straw apparel,
         a number of everyday garments and festival garments,
         chests and containers, some cooking and eating
         utensils, a number of pieces of jewelry, 20 smoking
         apparatuses, a fan and a mask. PHILIPPINE articles
         include some baskets, clothing, a number of everyday
         garments, containers, a number of jewelry pieces, a
         number of weapons, and a few musical instruments.
         The museum also has some BURMESE cooking and eating
         utensils, work tools and ritual objects, an everyday
         garment, containers, a number of jewelry pieces, some
         weapons, dieties and amulets, as well as a number
         of ritual and divining objects of TIBETAN origin.

         Dates: late 1700's to 1970's.

         95% catalogued; 5% or less photographed.   Small
         library.

         Hours: 9-5. Admission: $2.00 for adults, $6.00 for a
         family, $1.50 for seniors, $1.00 youths, under 7 free.

         Does not lend materials. Collection and library is
         open to researchers by appointment.

                              * * *

MA50   BOSTON PUBLIC LIBRARY, PRINT DEPARTMENT

         P.O. Box 286
         Boston, MA 02117
         (617) 536-5400 ext. 280

         Melinda Scanlon, Reference Librarian
         Staff: 4 permanent, 1 volunteer

         In the Boston Herald Traveler (1920-1972) photo morgue
         are numerous 8 X 10 glossies of CHINESE, JAPANESE,
         KOREAN, PHILIPPINE and VIETNAMESE ethnic subjects.
         The library has 20-30 tinted photographs of Japanese
         ethnic subjects.

MA50   (Boston Public Library, Print Department)
cont.
        Dates: 1920-1972.

        Hours: M-F 9-5.

        Lends materials to museums and galleries. Collection
        can be used by researchers by appointment. Fees for
        use of print department material include $10.00 per
        item published in a book or newspaper. More for other
        items.

                            * * *

MA51   PEABODY MUSEUM OF SALEM

        East India Square
        Salem, MA 09170
        (617) 745-1876

        Susan Bean, Curator of Ethnology

        The Peabody Museum maintains a large collection of
        approx. 75,000 East and Southeast Asian materials.

        Dates: mostly 19th and mid-20th c.

        100% catalogued; 90-100% photographed. Library.

        Hours: M-Sat 10-5, Sun 1-5. Admission: adults
        $3.50.

        Lends to other institutions. Library and collection
        can be used by researchers.

                            * * *

MA52   YESTERYEARS MUSEUM

        Box 609
        Sandwich, MA 02563
        (617) 888-2788

        Eilee M. Fair, Curator
        Staff: 2 (May-Oct. additional) permanent, 5-10
        volunteer

        This museum displays miniatures, the folk art of
        representations of architecture and furnishings of
        various cultures and historical periods. Besides
        American and European houses and furnishings,
        JAPANESE examples are well represented with many dolls
        and toys, some of which are customarily used for
        the Boys' and Girls' Day festivals, a 16th century
        scapegoat doll, kitchen utensils, decorative
        hangings, and tea ceremony articles. Especially
        notable is a Japanese toy palanquin of the Meiji era

                                        Massachusetts

MA52   (Yesteryears Museum)
cont.
        with oxen and figures. The museum also has a small
        collection of Japanese puppets and INDONESIAN
        wa-jang puppets, as well as CHINESE toy dolls, some
        in theatrical costume, and KOREAN items. Many of
        the museum's materials have been on display in
        recent exhibitions in Japan.

        Dates: 16th c. and late 19th and early 20th c.

        Display items photographed for personal files.

        Hours: May 1-Oct 31, M-Sat 10-4, Sun 1-4. Admission
        fees: $2.50 adults $2.00 seniors, $1.50 children.

        Does not ordinarily lend items. The collection can be
        used by researchers. The catalogue of a 1985
        centennial exhibition of miniatures sponsored by the
        Tokyo Gas Co. is available.

                              * * *

MI53   KALAMAZOO PUBLIC MUSEUM

        315 S. Rose St.
        Kalamazoo, MI 49007
        (616) 345-7092

        Lynn Houghton, Curator of Collections
        Staff: 10 permanent

        CHINESE items in this museum include a number of
        ceramic bottles, jars and pots, ceremonial garments,
        hats, jewelry, woodblock prints, masks, games and a
        collection of 22 musical instruments. The JAPANESE
        items include ceramicware, ceremonial garments,
        screens, kites, some musical instruments, and a number
        of dolls and toys. KOREAN ceramics and wooden
        containers, a large collection of PHILIPPINE baskets
        and woven hats and a large collection of THAI
        lacquerware are also maintained.

        Dates: 19th c. and unknown.

        100% catalogued; 40% photographed.

        Hours: T-Sat 9-5; Sun 1-5. Closed during summer. No
        fees.

                              * * *

MN54   MINNEAPOLIS INSTITUTE OF ARTS

        2400 Third Avenue South
        Minneapolis, MN 55404
        (612) 870-3214

MN54   (Minneapolis Institute of Arts)
cont.
         Robert Jacobsen, PhD, Curator of Asian Art
         Staff: 2 permanent in Asian Department

         CHINESE materials in the institute's possession
         include bamboo furniture, over 350 ceramicware
         pieces, 200 ceremonial garments, 200 decorative
         hangings, a few theatrical costumes, screens, and
         30 shadow puppets. JAPANESE materials include straw
         apparel, some teaware, some everyday garments,
         ceremonial garments, woodblock prints, screens,
         smoking apparatuses, and over 20 dolls and toys.
         Holdings also include KOREAN furniture and chests,
         a number of THAI ceramic pieces, and some VIETNAMESE
         objects.

         Dates: 19th c.

         20% photographed. Library.

         Hours: T-W, Sat 10-5; Th-F 10-9; Sun 12-5. Fees:
         $2.00 adults.

         Does not lend materials. Library and collection can
         be used by researchers.

                              * * *

MO55   MUSEUM OF ANTHROPOLOGY

         100 Swallow Hall
         University of Missouri-Columbia
         Columbia, MO 65201

         Dr. Elsebet Rowlett, Curator
         Staff: 2 permanent, 3 volunteer, 5 student

         This anthropological museum possesses a large
         collection of Southeast Asian material culture,
         mostly of THAI, but also of INDONESIAN, MALAYSIAN,
         and VIETNAMESE origin. This collection includes
         25 baskets, 50 basketwork tools, 25 ceramic pieces,
         a number of cooking and eating utensils, 25 everyday
         garments and a number of ceremonial garments and
         cloths, several decorative hangings, some smoking
         apparatuses, 100 metal or wood work tools, a number
         of dolls and toys, 50 puppets, some fans and musical
         instruments, a number of amulets, and several deities.
         Other Asian cultures are also well-represented in the
         museum: CHINESE items include baskets, ceramics,
         cooking and eating utensils, everyday and festival
         garments, abacuses, smoking apparatuses, fans, a
         number of dolls and toys, some musical instruments,
         woodblock prints, amulets, a deity and a number of
         ritual and divining objects. JAPANESE objects
         include baskets, reed apparel, and work tools,

MO55   (Museum of Anthropology)
cont.
        some ceramicware, cooking and eating utensils,
        everyday and festival garments, decorative hangings,
        abacuses, a screen, metal work tools, a number of
        dolls and toys, fans, kites, <u>origami</u>, woodblock
        prints, votive paintings, several shrines, a deity,
        and masks. KOREAN materials include straw apparel
        and basketwork tools, everyday garments, cooking and
        eating utensils, metal work tools, and a deity.
        PHILIPPINE items include 20 baskets, some basketwork
        tools, ceramics, everyday garments, cooking and eating
        utensils, smoking apparatuses, and metal work tools.

        Dates: 1890-1940.

        100% catalogued; 1% photographed. Small library.

        Hours: T-F 8-5; Sat-Sun 12-5. No admission fees.

        Lends materials on a short term basis. Collection and
        library can be used by researchers by appointment.

                              * * *

MO56   MUSEUM OF ART AND ARCHAEOLOGY

        #1 Pickard Hall
        University of Missouri-Columbia
        Columbia, MO 65211
        (314) 882-3591

        Forrest McGill, Director and Curator of Asian Art
        Staff: 12 permanent, 100 volunteer

        Approximately 30% of the museum's collection of East
        and Southeast Asian holdings are of folk or ethnic
        culture. CHINESE materials include a glass, ceramic
        jars and pots, teaware and numerous fragments of
        pottery, other cooking and eating utensils, a large
        collection of ceremonial garments and decorative
        hangings, a chest and other wood, ivory, and
        lacquerware containers, some money, a number of belt
        attachments, weapons, seals, some puppets, some
        papercuts, some amulets and deities, a number of
        ritual and divining objects, a large collection of
        calligraphy and paintings, and some figures or
        figurines. JAPANESE materials include some
        ceramicware, some ceremonial garments and decorative
        hangings, a number of containers of various materials
        a number of <u>netsuke</u> figures, 48 <u>suba</u> pieces, 62
        printing blocks, 177 woodblock prints, some origami,
        deities, ritual objects, calligraphy, candlesticks,
        masks, and figurines. The museum also has in its
        possession some KOREAN dolls and toys, teaware and a
        screen, INDONESIAN straw apparel, ceremonial textiles
        and decorative hangings, containers, weapons, lamps,

MO56   (Museum of Art and Archaeology)
cont.

jewelry, several deities, a number of ritual objects,
calligraphy and paintings, masks, a number of figures,
figurines, and figural reliefs, CAMBODIAN ceramics,
deities, and a figure, as well as THAI, LAOTIAN, and
BURMESE deities.

Dates: 19th and 20th c.

90% catalogued; 100% photographed. Library.

Hours: Tu-F 8-5; Sat-Sun 12-5. No admission fees.

No loans. Collection and library can be used by
researchers by appointment.

* * *

MT57   MINERAL COUNTY MUSEUM AND HISTORICAL SOCIETY

Box 533
Superior, MT 59872
(406) 882-4626

Cathryn Strombo
Staff: 2 permanent

Has 1900 census document relating to a large
settlement of JAPANESE living in the area, mostly
working on the railroad. This important document
shows dates of arrivals and specific employment for
all ethnic groups in this silver mining and logging
area.

Dates: 1900.

Research fee: $5.00 per hour. Appointment necessary.

* * *

NH58   HOOD MUSEUM OF ART

Dartmouth College
Hanover, NH 03755
(603) 646-3109

Gregory C. Schwarz, Assistant Curator and Associate
Registrar
Staff: 17 permanent

60% of the museum's East and Southeast Asian holdings
are folk and ethnic materials. The PHILIPPINE
collection is particularly significant with 45 baskets
and a number of straw hats, a number of ceramic
materials, approx. 40 everyday objects, a few
ceremonial garments, a large number of cooking and
eating utensils and containers, 30 work tools and 30

NH58   (Hood Museum of Art)
cont.

weapons. CHINESE materials include a number of
baskets and hats, ceramicware, everyday and ceremonial
garments, decorative hangings and theatrical costumes,
cooking and eating utensils, a number of wood and
metal containers, some furniture, smoking apparatuses,
some work tools and a number of weapons, fans,
puppets, musical instruments, amulets, 30 deities,
ritual and divining objects, shrines, lanterns and
50 packets of traditional medicine. JAPANESE material
culture is represented by ceramicware, including a
number of teaware pieces, 27 ceremonial garments and
cloth, some decorative hangings, a large number of
wood and metalwork containers, cooking and eating
utensils, abacuses, smoking apparatuses, work tools,
a number of weapons, fans, 12 musical instruments,
10 deities, several masks, and one complete sedan
chair. Southeast Asian material culture is also
represented with BURMESE and THAI hats, INDONESIAN
puppets, BALI masks, as well as THAI artifacts
collected from 1894-1897 by the U.S. consul to Siam,
including 25 ceramic pieces, a number everyday
garments, wood and metal containers, 24 smoking
apparatuses, numerous work tools and a number
of weapons. The museum also has a some KOREAN
ceremonial garments and cloth.

Dates: ca. 1850 - 1960.

100% catalogued; 5-10% photographed. Small library.

Hours: M-F 8:30-4:30. No admission fee.

Does not lend materials. Researchers can use
collection and library by appointment. The Southeast
Asian material is not currently on exhibit but can be
viewed on request.

                        * * *

NJ59   THE NEWARK MUSEUM

49 Washington St.
P.O. Box 540
Newark, NJ 07101
(201) 596-6662

Valrae Reynolds, Curator of Oriental Collections
Staff: 85 permanent, 73 volunteer

Approximately 34% of the museum's East and Southeast
Asian holdings may be considered folk or ethnic
material culture. The cultures represented in this
part of the museum's collection include CHINESE,
JAPANESE, KOREAN, PHILIPPINE, and INDONESIAN.

NJ59   (The Newark Museum)
cont.

Dates: 19th-20th centuries.

90% catalogued; 10% photographed. Library.

Hours: Tu-Sun 12-5. Admission free.

Does not lend materials, but collection and library
may be used by researchers.

* * *

NM60   MUSEUM OF INTERNATIONAL FOLK ART

P.O. Box 2087
Santa Fe, NM 87504-2087
(505) 827-8350

Karen Duffy, Curator and Coordinator Girard Collection
Catalog Project
Nora Fisher, Curator of Textiles
Staff: 23 permanent, over 100 volunteer

The Asian collections in this folk art museum are
extensive, containing nearly 10,000 objects,
especially textiles and costumes. The collections
reflect contemporary, as well as past folk or popular
life in the nations of the items' origin. The
JAPANESE collection, mostly donated by Alexander
Girard and Mrs. Charles Meech, has over 2400 items,
some from the AINU culture. These include 150-200
religious and ceremonial objects, 650 figural pieces,
over 500 toys, over 500 dolls-- some for the Boys' and
Girls' Days (see Festivals), over 100 miscellaneous
household goods, over 50 folk prints and paintings,
over 100 costume and textile pieces, 75 textile
fabrication tools, a number of boxes and containers,
baskets, pottery, jewelry, musical instruments, masks,
and puppets, as well as some furniture and items of
personal gear. CHINESE materials, many of which are
from the Caroline Bieber collection, include 750
festival prints and paintings, 245 papercuts, 200
costumes and textiles, over 100 votive offerings,
similar numbers of figurative pieces, toys, dolls and
household goods, a significant collection of large and
finely detailed shadow puppets from Szechwan, some
baskets, boxes and other containers, pottery, jewelry,
furniture, tools, and personal and animal gear.
KOREAN material culture is represented by over 50
pottery pieces, a number of miscellaneous household
goods and folk prints and paintings, as well as toys,
dolls, jewelry, boxes and containers, baskets and
personal gear. In the museum's possession are also
Southeast Asian materials: BURMESE figurative pieces,
toys, dolls, puppets, masks, musical instruments,
religious and ceremonial objects, household goods,

New Jersey-New Mexico

NM60   (Museum of International Folk Art)
cont.

boxes and containers and personal gear; THAI
figurative pieces, toys, masks, religious and
ceremonial objects, folk prints and paintings,
puppets, household goods, tools, and personal gear;
INDONESIAN folk prints and paintings, toys, masks,
religious and ceremonial objects, musical instruments,
jewelry, baskets, boxes and containers, household
goods, tools, personal gear, and a large collection
of over 500 puppets. The museum is actively
acquisitioning other pieces of Asian folk art.

Dates: late 19th and 20th centuries.

98% catalogued; 5% photographed. Library.

Hours: M-F 8-5. Admission fees: adults $3.00;
ages 6-16 $1.25.

Lends materials from the collection. The collection
and library are accessible to researchers by
appointment. The museum offers instructional
workshops for children.

                    * * *

NY61   THE BROOKLYN MUSEUM

200 Eastern Parkway
Brooklyn, NY 11238
(718) 638-5000

Robert Moes, Curator of Oriental Art

The Brooklyn Museum maintains an extensive collection
of JAPANESE folk art, OKINAWAN art and AINU artifacts.
Much of the Japanese folk art collection was gathered
by Stewart Culin on trips to Japan in 1909 and 1913-14
when many of the articles were still in everyday use.
The Ainu artifacts acquired by the museum in 1912 are
from the Frederick Starr collection. The folk arts
represented in this collection include folk paintings,
sculpture, ceramics, furniture, textiles, wooden
utensils, ironware, brass and copper work, signboards,
lacquer, basketry, weaving and dyeing, leather and
paper work, papier mâché masks, and toys. The museum
also has CHINESE, KOREAN, THAI, CAMBODIAN, PHILIPPINE
and VIETNAMESE folk art in its ethnographic
collections.

Dates: mainly 18th and 19th centuries; Japanese
Edo (1615-1868) and Meiji (1868-1912).

Hours: Daily 10-5, closed Tu. Admission fees: adults
$3.00, students $1.50, seniors and children $1.00.

NY61   (The Brooklyn Museum)
cont.

The publication by Robert Moes, <u>Mingei: Japanese Folk Art from the Brooklyn Museum Collection</u>, 1985, contains descriptions of over 120 items in the collection.

* * *

NY62   AMERICAN MUSEUM OF IMMIGRATION

Statue of Liberty, N.M.
Liberty Island
New York, NY 10004

Diana Pardue, Curator
Staff: 7 permanent, 1 volunteer

Although Ellis Island was not the main entry point for Asian immigrants to the United States, the immigration museum has some CHINESE and JAPANESE materials. The Chinese objects include cups and bowls, iron work tools, clay buildings, some prints and books, and writing instruments, as well as a vase, a necklace, a knife and sheath, a fan, a carved lichee seed and a lantern. The museum also has a number of photographs of Chinese subjects and a collection of Japanese coins.

Dates: unknown.

100% catalogued. Library.

Hours: Daily 9-5. No fees.

Does not lend. Library and collection can be used by researchers.

* * *

NY63   COOPER-HEWITT MUSEUM

2 East 91st Street
New York, NY 10128-9990
(212) 860-6960

David McFadden, Curator of Decorative Arts
Lillian Clagett, Technician, Drawings and Prints Dept.

Decorative Arts maintains a large collection of JAPANESE sword fittings, CHINESE ceramics, snuff bottles, and puppets, and some KOREAN and PHILIPPINE objects.

Drawings and Prints has CHINESE stencils for fabrics, drawings for furniture, pattern books, watercolor drawings of family and funeral scenes, puppets, and

NY63   (Cooper-Hewitt Museum)
cont.
        papercuts, JAPANESE stencils for fabrics, pattern
        books, puppets, <u>origami</u> and woodblock prints.

        Dates: 17-20th centuries.

        90% in Decorative Arts catalogued; 25% photographed.
        Almost all of the materials in Drawings and Prints
        are catalogued; very little photographed. Drawings
        and Prints has library.

        Does not lend materials. Library and collection may
        be used by researchers.

                            * * *

NY64   NEW YORK CHINATOWN HISTORY PROJECT

        Center for Community Studies
        70 Mulberry Street, 2nd Floor
        New York, NY 10013
        (212) 691-4785

        Charles Lai
        Staff: several volunteer

        The Project is an educational organization dedicated
        to reconstructing the 100 year history of New York
        Chinatown. With the largest collection of CHINESE
        American materials on the East Coast, it organizes
        oral history projects and bilingual exhibits and
        produces slide shows and documentary radio and
        video programs. Recent exhibitions include "Eight
        Pound Livelihood," documenting the history of laundry
        workers in the United States, "Contemporary
        Photographs of New York Chinatown" and "Pear Garden in
        the West--America's Chinese Theater, 1853-1983." The
        project center also provides a walking tour of
        Chinatown which covers the general history of this
        Lower East Side community, using folkloric material
        acquired from oral history interviews and discussing
        structures of historical and architectural
        significance.

        Dates: 19th c. to present.

        Hours: Office open M-F 10-6; Gallery, Bookstore and
        Library open F-Sun 12-5.

        Library open to public. Rents documentary videos and
        photographic exhibits and sells radio programs and
        books. Publishes <u>Bu Gao Ban</u>, a newsletter with
        historical information and special articles. Tours
        should be booked in advance.

                            * * *

                                              New York

OH65   THE DAYTON ART INSTITUTE

        456 Belmonte Park North
        P.O. Box 941
        Dayton, OH 45401-0941

        Clarence W. Kelley, Curator of Asian Art
        Staff: ca. 33 permanent, 200 volunteer

        The institute maintains arts and ethnic materials from
        many East and Southeast Asian cultures. CHINESE
        materials include a large collection of ceramics,
        a few ceremonial garments and decorative hangings, a
        number of screens, smoking apparatuses, a number of
        musical instruments, and deities. The museum also has
        a large collection of JAPANESE ceramics and other
        Japanese objects, including a few ceremonial garments,
        a number of screens, smoking apparatuses, and deities.
        KOREAN culture is represented by a collection of
        ceramics.

        Dates: 19th-20th c.

        100% catalogued; very little photographed. Library.

        Library materials can be obtained through inter-
        library loan. Library and collection are accessible
        to researchers by appointment.

                                * * *

OH66   DENISON UNIVERSITY MUSEUM OF ART

        Denison University
        Granville, OH
        (614) 587-6255

        Contact the registrar
        Staff: 1 permanent, student assistants

        A fine arts museum, the Denison University museum
        specializes in textiles, Buddhist sculpture,
        lacquerware and silver. Approximately 50% of the
        museum's East and Southeast Asian holdings are
        ethnographical materials. In addition to fine
        lacquerware and silver, the BURMESE collection
        contains over 300 tribal costumes, a number of
        everyday and ceremonial garments, a few decorative
        hangings, 200 pieces of straw wearing apparel,
        40 pieces of silverware, 200 pieces of lacquerware,
        a screen, a puppet, harps, and a Jataka parabaik
        of 1875. CHINESE items of material culture include
        25 ceremonial garments and 200 decorative hangings,
        mainly robes and embroidery patterns from the
        collection of Dr. Daniel Dye.

        Dates: Burmese 1844-1960; Chinese 18th-20th c.

OH66   (Denison University Museum of Art)
cont.
         100% catalogued; 10% photographed. College library.

         Hours: 10-4 during terms, no summer hours. No
         admission fee.

         Does not lend textiles. Books available through
         inter-library loan. Collection can be used by
         researchers.

                              * * *

OR67   SOUTHERN OREGON HISTORICAL SOCIETY

         P.O. Box 480
         Jacksonville, OR 97530
         (503) 899-1847

         Paul Richardson, Librarian/Archivist
         Staff: 4 permanent, 2 volunteer

         Founded in 1946, the Southern Oregon Historical
         Society collects, preserves, exhibits and interprets
         the history of Jackson County and Southern Oregon, a
         district settled mainly by miners from California in
         the early 1850's. The society has approximately 200
         black and white photographs of CHINESE immigrants
         from the 1850's-1880's, as well as miscellaneous
         documents and oral history tapes representing Chinese
         American life.

         Dates: mainly 1850's-1880's.

         Hours: Tu-Sat 1-5. Library collection open to public
         free of charge. Fees for research and reproduction
         services.

         Does not lend materials. Photographic reproduction
         and photocopy service available. Offers research
         services.

                              * * *

OR68   KAM WAH CHUNG AND CO. MUSEUM

         City Park NW Canton
         HCR 56 Box 290
         John Day, OR 97845
         (503) 575-1867

         Carolyn Micnhimer
         Staff: 1 permanent

         Originally a trading post on the Dalles Military Road,
         the museum houses thousands of artifacts and relics
         from the time of its use (1887-1940's) by two CHINESE

OR68   (Kam Wah Chung and Co. Museum)
cont.

immigrants from Kuangtung, Doc Ing Hay and Lung On.
Displays from the general store include mining
supplies, canned goods, notions, tobacco, and smoking
apparatuses. In the medical office of Doc Hay who was
an herbal doctor famous from Seattle to San Francisco,
more than 1,000 herbs, some of them rare, as well as
Chinese and Western medicines and prescriptions are on
display. Hay's bedroom contains the original
furniture, his clothing and personal items. The
kitchen contains bunks, antique furniture, a large
wood stove and both Chinese and Western cooking
utensils and foodstuffs, as well as gambling pieces.
A major shrine and several smaller ones, along with
many religious objects, illustrate the building's use
as a religious center for the Chinese community in
Eastern Oregon.

Dates: 1887-1940.

100% catalogued; 50% photographed. Library.

Hours: Sat and Sun 1-5; M-Th 9-12, 1-5.

Does not lend materials. Library and collection can
be used by researchers by appointment.

Cf. KAM WAH CHUNG COMPANY BUILDING, OR140
    KAM WAH CHUNG DAYS, OR181.

                         * * *

OR69   OREGON HISTORICAL SOCIETY

         1230 SW Park Avenue
         Portland, OR 97205
         (503) 222-1741

         Louis Flannery, Librarian

         Since 1956 the archives of the historical society has
         been collecting and preserving historic film footage.
         It now has a major collection of photographs, films
         and videotapes on Asian Americans, as well as on Asian
         countries. Among these is a major collection of
         PHILIPPINE Spanish-American War materials consisting
         of 1000 photographs, 8 albums, 12 photographs in the
         computer system and a number of documents. The
         society's CHINESE materials include 200 photographs in
         files and 120 in the computer system, 25 documents
         from the 1870's to the present, including the Kam Wah
         Chung collection, 7 video tapes, and 10 16mm films.
         JAPANESE materials include 100 photographs in files,
         214 in the computer system, 20 manuscripts, mostly
         from the 1940's, and 20 16mm films. KOREAN materials
         include 4 photographs in the computer system and a

OR69   (Oregon Historical Society)
cont.
        16mm film. The library also has 16mm films on
        VIETNAMESE, THAI and KAMPUCHIAN subjects, a 1966 photo
        of an Oregon Buddhist Church, and a collection of
        books on Chinese, Japanese and Southeast Asian ethnic
        subjects.

        The associated museum has 55 Chinese articles, 10 WWII
        Japanese articles, and 75 Philippine items, mostly
        Spanish-American War souvenirs.

        Dates: 1870's to present.

        Hours: M-Sat 10-4:45. Fees: viewing table rental fee
        $5.00 per hour; research fee $25.00 per hour.

        Collections are available to the public for research.
        Appointment suggested. Society also offers
        reproduction, research and preservation services.

        Cf. KAM WAH CHUNG AND CO. MUSEUM, OR68.

                            * * *

PA70   BALCH INSTITUTE FOR ETHNIC STUDIES

        18 South 7th St.
        Philadelphia, PA 19106
        (215) 925-8090

        R. Joseph Anderson, Library Director
        Staff: 5 permanent, 8 volunteer

        In the archives of the institute are materials which
        document the history and ethnic life of several Asian
        American ethnic groups: 117 photographs, 18 broadsides
        and numerous documents and books on CHINESE ethnic
        culture; 196 photographs, 21 broadsides, numerous
        documents and a large collection of books on JAPANESE
        ethnic culture; 26 photographs and over 20 books on
        KOREAN ethnic culture; 24 photographs and some
        documents and books on HMONG and VIETNAMESE cultures;
        and broadsides and books on PHILIPPINE immigrant
        culture. The archives also provides guides,
        resources and teachers' training manuals.

        The museum has materials representing several of these
        ethnic cultures: CHINESE straw apparel, 25-50 pieces
        of everyday clothing including shoes, ceremonial
        garments, decorative hangings, eyeglass cases, cooking
        and eating utensils, dolls and toys, fans, kites, and
        puppets; JAPANESE everyday garments, theatrical
        costumes, containers, furniture, screens, musical
        instruments, shell jewelry, umbrellas, and a number
        of toys and dolls; and VIETNAMESE and HMONG everyday
        garments and decorative hangings.

PA70   (Balch Institute for Ethnic Studies)
cont.
        Dates: 1900-present.

        Hours: 9-5. No fees.

        Does not lend materials. Library and material culture
        collection can be used by researchers by appointment.
        Publishes a newsletter: New Dimensions. Has sponsored
        special exhibitions on Asian American themes.

                            * * *

TN71   CHEEKWOOD BOTANICAL GARDENS AND FINE ARTS CENTER

        Forrest Park Drive
        Nashville, TN 37205
        (615) 352-8632

        Susan W. Knowles, Curator of Collections
        Charlotte Brailsford, Registrar
        Staff: 9 permanent, approx. 200 volunteer

        The museum's East and Southeast Asian materials
        include both ethnographical and export craft items of
        CHINESE, JAPANESE and INDONESIAN provenance. Most
        significant of these materials is the 350 piece
        collection of Oriental snuff bottles on display in a
        permanent exhibition. The Indonesian materials
        include puppets, a musical instrument, and a number
        of masks.

        Dates: Indonesian materials-20th century.

        Minimally catalogued. Library.

        Inter-library loan. Collection and library are
        accesible to researchers.

                            * * *

TX72   MUSEUM OF ORIENTAL CULTURES

        426 S. Staples
        Corpus Christie, TX 78401
        (512) 883-1303

        Pat Bacak-Clements, Curator
        Staff: 5 permanent, 30 volunteer

        Approximately 30% of the museum's East and Southeast
        Asian materials are folk or ethnic. CHINESE materials
        include a few everyday garments and theatrical
        costumes, some wood and metalwork containers, dolls
        and toys, musical instruments, and deities. The
        JAPANESE materials include some baskets, a large
        collection of bottles, jars and pots, as well as other

                                Pennsylvania-Tennessee-Texas

TX72   (Museum of Oriental Cultures)
cont.

ceramic pieces, about 20 everyday garments and 20
decorative hangings, 50 cooking and eating utensils,
containers, a number of paper screens, a number of
dolls and toys, 30 fans, a few kites, a number of
puppet heads, contemporary origami, 20 deities, a
shrine, a number of lanterns, and 30 reproductions of
masks. The museum also has a few KOREAN, PHILIPPINE
and MALAYSIAN articles.

Dates: 1900 to present.

50% catalogued. Library.

Hours: Tu-Sat 10-4. Admission: adults $1.00,
seniors .75, students .50, children .35.

Does not lend materials. Materials are available to
the public for in-museum use during regular hours.

* * *

TX73   INSTITUTE OF TEXAN CULTURES

801 S. Bowie
P.O. Box 1226
San Antonio, TX 78294

Clare Bass, Reference Librarian
Tom Shelton, Photo Librarian
Phyllis McKenzie, Curator of Collections
Staff: 125 permanent, approx. 400 volunteer

Focusing on folk and ethnic materials, the Institute
of Texan cultures has photographs of several Asian
American ethnic groups: 250 photographs of CHINESE
subjects, 300 photographs of JAPANESE subjects, and 60
photographs and 100 color slides of PHILIPPINE
subjects. The library also has documents of Chinese
and Japanese American history, as well as oral history
tapes of Chinese, Japanese, VIETNAMESE and KHMER
immigrants. On display are the following items of
material culture: Chinese cooking and eating utensils,
a few dolls and toys, a number of musical instruments,
a banner, a few ritual and divining objects, a few
masks and a rickshaw. The Japanese materials include
36 everyday garments, a military patch, some straw
apparel, some dolls and toys, fans, and work tools.
The Philippine materials include some baskets and
straw clothing, a shield, some mats, some everyday
garments, some ceremonial garments and cloth, a flag,
cooking and eating utensils, containers, smoking
apparatuses, a few work tools, weapons, a number of
dolls and toys, a few fans, huts, some carvings, and
medicine glasses.

Texas

TX73   (Institute of Texan Cultures)
cont.
         Date: 20th c.

         All objects accessioned and photographed; not
         catalogued. Library.

         Hours: Tu-Sun 9-5. No admission fees. $1.00 parking
         fee.

         Does not lend material culture items, but books can be
         borrowed through inter-library loan. Vertical file
         material can be photocopied and photographs can be
         printed. Both library and material culture collection
         may be used by researchers.

                              * * *

VA74   REUEL B. PRITCHETT MUSEUM

         Bridgewater College
         Bridgewater, VA 22812
         (703) 828-2501

         Thelma S. Replogle, Director
         Staff: 1 permanent

         Housing the collection of Reuel B. Pritchett, a Church
         of the Brethern preacher, and materials donated by
         other persons, the museum has a small collection of
         CHINESE articles, including cups, bowls and plates,
         teaware, a few ceremonial garments, a decorative
         hanging, abacuses, a screen, a smoking apparatus, a
         shoe, and dolls and toys, as well as various
         PHILIPPINE articles, including baskets, work tools and
         a collection of 30 war implements.

         Dates: 1913-1945

         100% catalogued.

         No loans. Collection accessible by appointment.

                              * * *

VA75   DANVILLE MUSEUM OF FINE ARTS AND HISTORY

         975 Main St.
         Danville, VA 24541
         (804) 793-5644

         Mr. Bill Corr, Gallery Manager
         Staff: 4 permanent, 4 volunteer

         Hours: Tu-F 10-5; Sun 2-5. No admission fee.

         The Danville Museum has a small collection of CHINESE
         material culture, including ceramics, decorative

VA75   (Danville Museum of Fine Arts and History)
cont.
         hangings, a number of dolls and toys, a few fans and a
         few pieces of festival calligraphy. It also maintains
         a very small collection of KOREAN woodblock prints and
         festival painting.

         Dates: 1700-1950.

         100% catalogued; 100% photographed.

         Hours: Tu-F 10-5; Sun 2-5. No admission fees.

         Conditional lending. Collection may be used by
         researchers by appointment.

                              * * *

WA76   WASHINGTON STATE UNIVERSITY MUSEUM OF ANTHROPOLOGY

         Department of Anthropology
         Washington State University
         Pullman, WA 99164
         (509) 335-3936

         Eric H. Wood, Teaching Assistant

         Approximately 65% of the museum's collection is of
         East and Southeast Asian ethnological materials.
         PHILIPPINE materials include a few baskets, teaware,
         everyday garments, decorative hangings, bark cloth,
         cooking and eating utensils, containers, smoking
         apparatuses, work tools, wooden combs, projectile
         points, dolls and toys, fans, musical instruments,
         a carving and photographs. The CHINESE materials
         include a number of deities, shrines and four cases of
         materials representing religious and festival arts.
         VIETNAMESE materials include a basket and fishtrap,
         smoking apparatuses, and work tools. The museum also
         has JAPANESE, RYUKYU ISLAND, and INDONESIAN materials.

         Dates: unknown.

         95% catalogued.

         Collection accessible to researchers by appointment.

                              * * *

WA77   HENRY ART GALLERY

         University of Washington, DE 15
         Seattle, WA 98195
         (206) 543-2281

WA77   (Henry Art Gallery)
cont.
        Judy Sourakli, Curator of Collections
        Staff: 9 permanent, several volunteer

        The Henry Art Gallery preserves the University of
        Washington's collection of fine arts and textiles.
        About 60-65% of the collection is composed of East and
        Southeast Asian ethnographic objects. The textile
        collection emphasizes hand-woven and hand-decorated
        costumes and textiles, including a major collection of
        INDIAN textiles. CHINESE textiles, numbering
        approximately 700, include some bedding, a large
        number of everyday and ceremonial garments, shoes,
        embroidered sleeve bands and decorative hangings.
        Other Chinese materials include puppets and votive
        paintings. JAPANESE textiles, numbering about
        500 items, include many everyday garments, some
        priests' robes, samples of resist-dye techniques and
        some decorative hangings. Other Japanese articles
        include a large collection of modern folk pottery, a
        number of dolls and some fans. The gallery also has
        INDONESIAN examples of the art of batik and everyday
        and ceremonial garments, KOREAN ceramics and straw
        apparel, and some PHILIPPINE everyday garments.

        Dates: early 20th c.-1960's.

        100% catalogued; 100% photographed.

        Hours: Tu-F 10-5; Th evening 5-7; Sat-Sun 11-5.
        Admission: general $2.00, students and seniors $1.00,
        members and children free.

        Lends to other museums. The collection can be used by
        researchers by appointment. Relevant library
        materials can be consulted in the Southeastern Asia
        Division of the University of Washington Library.

                            * * *

WI78   KENOSHA PUBLIC MUSEUM

        5608 10th Ave.
        Kenosha, WI 53140
        (414) 656-8026

        Paula Touhey, Director
        Staff: 5 permanent, 12 volunteer

        CHINESE items in the museum include a large collection
        of ivory carvings, a number of ceramics, some everyday
        and ceremonial garments, some containers, a few pieces
        of furniture, some fans, and deities. JAPANESE items
        include ivory carvings, a number of ceramics, some
        everyday and ceremonial garments, a number of fans,
        30 woodblock prints and a few lanterns.

WI78   (Kenosha Public Museum)
cont.
        Dates: 1400-present.

        100% catalogued; 1% photographed. Library.

        Hours: M-F 9-5; Sat 9-12; Sun 1-4. No fees.

        Does not lend materials. Library and collection can
        be used by researchers by appointment.

                              * * *

WI79   VITERBO COLLEGE MUSEUM COLLECTIONS

        Viterbo College
        815 S. 9th St.
        La Crosse, WI 54601
        (608) 784-0040

        Sister Joyce Conwell
        Staff: 1 permanent

        90% of the college's East and Southeast Asian holdings
        are ethnographic materials from which special exhibits
        are made. These include CHINESE basketwork tools and
        mats, ceramics, bedding, 40-50 everyday garments,
        20-25 ceremonial garments, 50-60 decorative hangings,
        theatrical costumes, abacuses, chests, cooking and
        eating utensils, wood and metal containers and work
        tools, 25 pieces of furniture, smoking apparatuses,
        work tools, numerous dolls and toys, fans, a number of
        musical instruments, papercuts, amulets, deities,
        ritual and divining objects, shrines, a number of
        votive paintings, festival calligraphy and painting,
        lanterns, masks, wood carvings showing Chinese social
        customs, and ivory and jade carvings. JAPANESE
        material culture is represented by various ceramic
        pieces, a number of everyday garments, some ceremonial
        garments, some decorative hangings, a theatrical
        costume, cooking and eating utensils, a number of wood
        and metal containers and work tools, some furniture, a
        number of dolls and toys, 20-25 fans, papercuts, a few
        shrines and ritual objects, some minga (votive
        paintings), festival calligraphy and carvings. KOREAN
        textiles and costumes, furniture, dolls and toys, a
        musical instrument and religious shrines, PHILIPPINE
        basketwork, textiles and costumes, cooking and eating
        utensils, fans, woodblock prints, and religious
        objects, and some INDONESIAN, MALAYSIAN and VIETNAMESE
        materials are also in the museum's possession.

        Dates: Late 1800's to present.

        100% catalogued; 5% photographed. Library with some
        related materials.

WI79   (Viterbo College Museum Collections)
cont.
        Hours: M-F 7-11. No admission fees.

        Lends materials. The collection and library may be
        used by researchers by appointment.

                            * * *

WI80   HELEN ALLEN TEXTILE COLLECTION

        1300 Linden Drive
        University of Wisconsin
        Madison, WI 53706
        (608) 262-1162

        Blenda Femenias, Curator
        Staff: 2 permanent, 2-4 volunteer

        In this major collection of textiles and costumes from
        around the world, 60-70% of the Asian materials are
        ethnographic textiles; the remaining pieces are
        export products. The CHINESE ethnographic materials
        include a number of everyday and ceremonial garments,
        some decorative hangings, and a number of theatrical
        costumes. JAPANESE materials include everyday and
        festival garments. INDONESIAN articles include 50
        everyday garments, 25 ceremonial garments or cloth
        pieces, and other miscellaneous textiles. Also in the
        museum's collection are some KOREAN everyday garments.
        The basis of the collection was donated to the
        university by Helen Louise Allen, a teacher at the
        University of Wisconsin at Madison from 1927-1968.

        Dates: 1860's to present; majority is 20th century.

        80% catalogued; 100% photographed. Small library.
        Laser videodisc available.

        Hours: M-F 9-4 or by appointment. No admission fees.
        Charge for photos, computer searches etc.

        Does not lend materials. Collection and library, as
        well as videodisc, can be used by researchers.

                            * * *

WY81   WYOMING STATE ARCHIVES AND HISTORICAL DEPARTMENT

        Barrett Building
        Cheyenne, WY 82002
        (307) 777-7031

        Paula West Chavoya, Supervisor of Hist. Photographs

        Maintains a collection of black and white photographs
        of CHINESE labourers in Wyoming from 1890-95.

                                        Wisconsin-Wyoming

WY81   (Wyoming State Archives and Historical Department)
cont.
        Dates: 1890-1895.

        Hours: M-F 8-5. No admission fees.

        Does not lend materials. Collection may be used by
        researchers by appointment.

                            * * *

WY82   SWEETWATER COUNTY HISTORICAL MUSEUM

        80 West Flaming Gorge Way
        Green River, WY 92935
        (307) 875-2611 Ext. 263

        Henry F. Chadey, Director
        Staff: 3 permanent

        This historical museum has materials from the mining
        period in Wyoming, including CHINESE baskets,
        ceramicware, cooking and eating utensils, bedding,
        a number of everyday garments, a few decorative
        hangings, flags, abacuses, some smoking apparatuses,
        work tools, weapons, jewelry, a fan, some musical
        instruments, 100 game pieces, a deity, prayer beads,
        figurines, and 50 photographs, as well as JAPANESE
        baskets, bedding and garments.

        Dates: 19th c.

        100% catalogued.

        Hours: M-F 9-4:30; extended hours in May and August.
        No admission fees.

        Does not lend articles. Collection may be used by
        researchers by appointment.

                            * * *

BC83   BURNABY VILLAGE MUSEUM

        4900 Deer Lake Ave.
        Burnaby, BC V5G 3T6
        (604) 294-1231

        Staff: 10 permanent

        Most Asian immigrants to Canada settled at first in
        the province of British Columbia where they were hired
        to construct railroad lines, or to work in mines and
        lumber mills inland and in coastal fish canneries.
        This open air historical village has thirty
        buildings illustrating life in British Columbia

BC83   (Burnaby Village Museum)
cont.

from 1890-1925. A CHINESE herbal shop and a JAPANESE
bath or <u>ofuro</u> represent the lives of Asian immigrants
to the area. The Chinese herbal shop, a combination
of two separate stores founded in Victoria around 1900
and reconstructed 2/3 scale at the museum in 1971,
served the medicinal needs of Chinese settlers, mainly
miners and railway workers. The interior of the shop
has carved frescoed cabinets with drawers for herbs,
glass-fronted cabinets, shop counters, containers with
mixed dry and liquid contents, and herbs and roots, as
well as instruments used for weighing, grinding and
mixing. Also located in the shop are sewing baskets,
textiles, cooking utensils, 100 herbal crates, an
abacus, a waterpipe, work tools, general merchandise,
such as chopsticks, chinaware, and spices, a mail rack
and materials for making and serving tea to costumers.
The Japanese <u>ofuro</u> built in 1977 by the Japanese-
Canadian Citizens Association commemorates the 100th
anniversary of the arrival of the first known Japanese
settler in Canada. It illustrates a type of cedar
bath house used by Japanese in logging camps, mining
towns, and canneries in British Columbia the last
quarter of the 19th century.

Dates: early 1900's.

Hours: 11-4:30 daily or by appointment.

                          * * *

BC84   CUMBERLAND MUSEUM

First and Dunsmuir Ave.
P.O. Box 258
Cumberland, BC   VOR 1SO
(604) 336-2445

Dale Reeves, Museum Manager and Curator
Staff: 1 permanent, 14 volunteer

The town of Cumberland flourished as a coal mining
town, and artifacts in the museum tell the settlement
history. CHINESE materials in the museum include some
baskets, straw tools, over 200 pieces of ceramicware,
some everyday garments and decorative hangings, a few
abacuses, chests, wood and metal containers,
furniture, over 30 cooking and eating utensils,
25-30 smoking apparatuses, some metal work tools and
a brass counterweight, some carved stone figurines,
some fans, some musical instruments, folk paintings,
gambling chips, artists' tools, deities, a number of
ritual and divining objects, shrines, calligraphic
scrolls and paintings, some lanterns, curing articles
and instructions, pill boxes, medicine bottles,
medicine, oil, personal stamps and seals, approx.

                                    British Columbia

BC84   (Cumberland Museum)
cont.
        600 coins and bills, newspapers and magazines.
        Especially significant is the museum's collection
        of 50 letters, a large number of envelopes and various
        cards, newspapers, magazines, records and books.
        JAPANESE materials include a large number of bottles,
        jars, pots, over 20 cups, bowls, plates, teaware,
        a ceramic bell, a number of festival and everyday
        garments, a fire balloon, some cooking and eating
        utensils, a number of screens and scrolls, ritual
        objects, newspapers, magazines and various records.
        The museum also maintains a special collection of
        approximately 750 glass negatives taken in the local
        area between 1909 and 1929 by three Japanese Canadian
        photographers. 60% of this collection is of Japanese
        subjects and 10% of Chinese subjects.

        Dates: 1860-1942.

        95% catalogued. Small library.

        Hours: April-Oct, daily 9-5. Admission fees: adults
        $2.00, seniors $1.00.

        Lends materials. Collection and library may be
        used by researchers by appointment. A book on the
        Cumberland Japanese by Miyoko Kudo is available in
        Japanese.

                          * * *

BC85   LANGLEY CENTENNIAL MUSEUM AND NATIONAL EXHIBITION
        CENTER

        Corner of Mavis and King Streets
        Box 800
        Fort Langley, BC VOX 1JO
        (604) 888-3922

        Warren Sommer, Curator
        Staff: 2.5 permanent, 35 volunteer

        Included in the museum's collection of CHINESE
        materials are a number of straw clothing pieces,
        baskets and work tools, 30 bottles, jars and pots,
        some ceramic cups and bowls, a vase, cooking and
        eating utensils, a number of medicine bottles,
        an herbalist's grinder, some everyday garments,
        a few festival garments and decorative hangings,
        abacuses, a chest, smoking apparatuses, and festival
        calligraphy. The museum also has some JAPANESE items
        including clothing and ceramicware, as well as an
        INDONESIAN cloth. A collection of 1500 photographs
        represents Central Fraser Valley History. The museum
        is now collecting "materials of excellence reflecting
        the area's increasingly multi-cultural character."

                                        British Columbia

BC85   (Langley Centennial Museum and National Exhibition
cont.   Center)

Dates: 1850-1920.

Hours: Tu-Sat 10-5; Sun 1-5. No admission fee.

100% catalogued. Small library.

Does not lend materials. Collection and library are
accessible to researchers by appointment.

* * *

BC86   FORT STEELE HERITAGE PARK

16 km NE of Cranbrook on Highway 93/95
Fort Steele, BC VJOB 1NO
(604) 489-3351

Derryll White, Museum Technician
Staff: 16 permanent, 60 volunteer

CHINESE miners' cabins and graveyard are maintained at
this turn of the century townsite. Chinese domestics
were employed at Fort Steele during its boom from
1896-1905. Chinese also ran laundries, restaurants,
commercial vegetable gardens and at least one drug
store and general store. The park also has about
100 photographs of mining, vegetable gardens and the
cemetery, local papers with comments on the Chinese
Exclusion Laws and a collection of approximately 25
bottles, jars and pots.

Dates: 1860-1915.

70% catalogued. Library with a few relevant
documents.

Hours: May-Oct 8-4; Nov-Apr phone for hours.

No loans. Library and collection may be used by
researchers by appointment.

* * *

BC87   GREENWOOD MUSEUM

Copper Street
Box 399
Greenwood, BC VOH 1JO
(604) 445-6355

Rosemary Santopiato, Curator

Greenwood, BC, once a mining town, became one of the
relocation points during WWII for ethnic JAPANESE who

British Columbia

BC87   (Greenwood Museum)
cont.
        were deported inland from the Canadian Pacific
        coastal areas. Many Japanese Canadians still reside
        in the area. The collection includes various Japanese
        articles, including miniature rain gear, decorative
        hangings, silk embroidery pictures, an abacus and a
        screen, writing instruments, art brushes, a box,
        wooden shoes, a number of dolls and toys, fans,
        a musical instrument, paper screens and scrolls,
        a shrine with ritual objects and festival calligraphy
        or painting. The museum also has a significant
        collection of 50-100 origami pieces. A print and
        photographic display describes the internment of the
        Japanese in Greenwood in 1942 and their subsequent
        settlement.

        Dates: 1900 on.

        100% catalogued; 100% photographed. Library.

        Hours: May-Oct 8-5. Admission fees: adults $1.00,
        students .50, children .25.

        No loans. The collection and library which has two
        research papers on Japanese Canadians may be used by
        researchers. Local public library has Japanese books
        for loan.

                        * * *

BC88   KETTLE RIVER MUSEUM

        Entwined Trees Park
        Box 149
        Midway, BC VOH 1MO
        (604) 449-2413 (Summer)

        Frances Elliott, Curator
        Staff: 2 permanent, 1 volunteer

        On the Canadian Pacific Railway route, the museum has
        farming, mining, and logging exhibitions, as well as
        JAPANESE articles, including ceramics, everyday
        garments, a fencing costume, soloban, some money
        pieces, cooking and eating utensils, a bamboo flower
        pot, work tools, a calligraphy set, a doll, fans, a
        paper banner (family crest), and cherry blossom
        sprays. Also has a few CHINESE smoking apparatuses.

        Dates: 1907 to 1972.

        100% catalogued; 10% photographed. Library.

        Hours: 10-4 daily, May 15th to Sept. 15. Admission
        fees: adult $1.00, seniors and students or by
        donation.

                                        British Columbia

BC88   (Kettle River Museum)
cont.
        Some materials available for loan. Library and
        collection can be used by researchers.

                        * * *

BC89   MISSION MUSEUM AND ARCHIVES

        33201 2nd Ave.
        Mission, BC V2V 1J9
        (604) 826-1011

        Dorothy Crosby, Curator
        Staff: volunteers

        The Mission Museum maintains a 1925 JAPANESE hall and
        church and has in its possession Japanese ceramics and
        screens. It also has CHINESE objects, including some
        ceramic pieces, a pair of pillows, a few pairs of
        sandals and shoes for bound feet, some smoking
        apparatuses, a few fans and a musical instrument.
        Photographs held include 40 of Japanese immigrants and
        buildings and a few photographs of buildings occupied
        by Chinese.

        Dates: early 1900's.

        50% photographed.

        Hours: M-F 10-4; Sat and Sun 2-4. No fees.

        Does not lend materials, but collection is accessible
        to researchers.

                        * * *

BC90   NANAIMO CENTENNIAL MUSEUM

        100 Cameron Road, Adjacent to Piper Park
        Nanaimo, BC V9R 2X1
        (604) 753-1821

        Shelley Harding, Education Co-ordinator
        Staff: 4 permanent, 15 volunteer

        Maintains a large collection of CHINESE material
        culture from the early settlement period, including
        20 baskets and a number of pieces of reed clothing,
        a large collection of over 100 ceramic pieces, 25-30
        cooking and eating utensils, a few containers, some
        furniture, bedding, 46 ceremonial and everyday
        garments, shop signs, abacuses, money, smoking
        apparatuses, fans, a musical instrument, mahjong
        gambling pieces, calligraphy, religious paper items,
        incense, paintings and prints, a lion's head and
        banner for processions, and 20 articles used by

                                    British Columbia

BC90   (Nanaimo Centennial Museum)
cont.
        herbalists, such as bottles, a bench, and instruments
        used for grinding and burning. The museum also
        maintains a few JAPANESE fishing articles and has a
        collection of 30 photographs of Chinese subjects and
        a few photographs of Japanese subjects.

        Dates: late 19th c.

        100% catalogued. Library.

        Hours: 9-5. No fees.

        Rarely lends materials. Library and collection may be
        used by researchers by appointment.

                            * * *

BC91   IRVING HOUSE HISTORIC CENTRE AND MUSEUM

        302 Royal Ave.
        New Westminster, BC V3L 1H7
        (604) 521-7656

        Archie W. Miller, Curator
        Staff: 2 permanent, 10 volunteer

        Irving House maintains CHINESE materials including
        straw slippers, ceramic shards from a demolished
        building, abacuses, scales, signs, papers and other
        miscellaneous items. It also has photographs of
        Chinese subjects.

        Dates: 1860's to 1970's.

        Hours: May-mid-Sept, Tu-Sun 11-5; mid-Sept-Apr,
        Sat-Sun 1-5. Admission fee: by donation.

        Does not lend materials, but researchers may view
        them. The collection is currently being rearranged
        and a history of the Chinese in New Westminster is
        being made. A slide programme and walking tour have
        been offered by the museum.

                            * * *

BC92   NORTH SHORE MUSEUM AND ARCHIVES

        209 W. 4th St.
        North Vancouver, BC VTM 1H8
        (604) 987-5618

        Shannon Martin
        Staff: permanent, 4 volunteer

BC92   (North Shore Museum and Archives)
cont.

The museum maintains items of CHINESE immigrant
material culture, including ceramics, teaware,
ceremonial garments and cloth, decorative hangings,
dolls and toys, red gift envelopes, lucky money,
and items of JAPANESE immigrant culture in a
collection of ceramics. The archives also has
historical photographs of both ethnic groups.

Dates: 1930-1980.

100% catalogued; 100% photographed.

Hours: 8:30-4:30. No admission fees.

* * *

BC93   PORT MOODY STATION MUSEUM

2734 Murray Street
Port Moody, BC V3H 1X2
(604) 939-1648

Diane Rogers, Curator
Staff: several volunteer

The museum at the site of a 1907 Canadian Pacific
Railway station features over 100 photographs of
CHINESE labourers in the C.P.R. construction lines
in BC 1881 to 1886, of JAPANESE in the local logging
camps, and of both Chinese and Japanese in the lumber
mills. The museum also has an exhibit of a 1927
Chinese general store patronized by lumber mill
workers in Port Moody. Chinese objects on display
include 42 bottles, 50 ceramic containers, 20 ceramic
eating and drinking items, a scale, a barrel and
other containers, a doll and a fan. Japanese objects
include 45 ceramic pieces and a wok.

Dates: 1900-1930's.

50% catalogued; 25% photographed. Library.

Hours: Weekends 1-8; Summer also on weekdays 1-8.

Lends materials on a limited basis. Library and
collection can be used by researchers.

* * *

BC94   PRINCETON AND DISTRICT MUSEUM AND ARCHIVES

167 Vermillion Avenue
P.O. Box 281
Princeton, BC V0X 1W0
(604) 295-7588

British Columbia

BC94   (Princeton and District Museum and Archives)
cont.
        Evelyn McCallum, President
        Staff: 3 volunteer

        The collection contains CHINESE artifacts, including
        baskets, work tools, a yoke, everyday garments, a bean
        grinder, a number of ceramic pieces, abacuses, some
        dolls and toys, papercuts, folk paintings and stone
        rubbings. Also in the museum's possession are KOREAN
        paintings, a PHILIPPINE pina shirt, MALAY clothing,
        batik pieces and a bronz figure, and an INDONESIAN
        screen and puppet.

        Dates: 1920's-unknown.

        100% catalogued.

        Hours: mid-June-Labour Day, daily 10-7. Fees: by
        donation.

        Lends materials. Collection is accessible to
        researchers by appointment.

                                * * *

BC95   REVELSTOKE MUSEUM AND ARCHIVES

        P.O. Box 1908
        Revelstoke, BC V0E 2S0
        (604) 837-3067

        Cathy English, Curator
        Staff: 1 permanant (2 additional in summer);
        2 volunteer

        Revelstoke maintains some CHINESE materials including
        teacups, medicinal balances for weighing herbal
        medicines, a small tablecloth and a banner, a wooden
        abacus, a large rice grinder and a small grindstone, a
        hookah, and a cymbal with lettering, as well as
        photographs showing Chinese businesses and merchants.
        The museum also has documents relating to the JAPANESE
        who worked on the Canadian Pacific Railway, including
        a memorial notice for 62 men killed in an avalanche,
        many of whom were Japanese.

        Dates: 1870-1930.

        100% catalogued.

        Hours: Summer, M-Sat 12-9; Winter, weekday afternoons.

        The collection is accessible to researchers by
        apppointment.

                                * * *

                                        British Columbia

BC96   CITY OF VANCOUVER ARCHIVES

       1150 Chestnut Street
       Vancouver, BC V6J 3J9
       (604) 736-8561

       Ken Young, Archivist
       Staff: 9 permanent, 3 volunteer

       Vancouver became one of the major urban settlements
       for CHINESE and JAPANESE in Canada. The city archives
       has significant material, including black and white
       stills, as well as manuscript collections, on the
       history of Chinese and Japanese immigration. The
       holdings on other Asian immigrant groups are limited.

       Hours: M-F 9:30-5:30. Photo reproduction fees only.

       Does not lend materials. No appointment needed for
       use by researchers.

* * *

BC97   UNIVERSITY OF BRITISH COLUMBIA LIBRARY, SPECIAL
       COLLECTIONS DIVISION

       Library, University of B.C.
       1956 Main Mall
       Vancouver, BC V6T 1Y3
       (604) 228-2521

       Anne Yandle, Head
       Staff: 8 permanent

       Special Collections at the University of British
       Columbia Library maintains many photographs, as well
       as oral history tapes on ethnic JAPANESE in Canada and
       has some photographs of ethnic CHINESE. It also holds
       documents and books on both groups of immigrants.

       Dates: 19th century to present.

       Collection is catalogued.

       Hours: M-F 9-5; Sat 12-5 when university is in
       session. No fees, except for copying.

       Does not lend materials. Collection can be used by
       researchers.

* * *

BC98   THE VANCOUVER MUSEUM

       1100 Chestnut Street
       Vancouver, BC V6J 3J9
       (604) 736-4431

BC98   (The Vancouver Museum)
cont.
        Robb Watt, Director
        Staff: 35-40 permanent, 170 volunteer

        Has significant holdings of Asian and Asian American
        objects of material culture. CHINESE materials,
        amounting to 2,331 artifacts, include some basketware,
        over 200 ceramic pieces, over 100 textiles and
        costumes, a few chests, some cooking and eating
        utensils, 28 containers, a few screens, 36 smoking
        apparatuses, a number of work tools, a number of
        censers, a number of wood and metal representations,
        dolls and toys, a number of fans, 27 musical
        instruments, amulets, a large collection of media of
        exchange, lanterns and other articles. JAPANESE
        materials, totalling 1,107 objects, include
        basketware, 45 ceramic pieces, 28 textile and costume
        articles, some chests, some cooking and eating
        utensils, 22 containers, a few screens, some smoking
        apparatuses, a few work tools and 400 other wood and
        metalwork items, 105 dolls and toys, a few fans, a
        number of musical instruments, a large collection of
        coins and other items. KOREAN, PHILIPPINE,
        INDONESIAN, MALAYSIAN, VIETNAMESE, LAOTIAN, THAI and
        BURMESE objects of material culture are also in the
        museum's possession.

        Dates: 1766 BC to present.

        90-95% catalogued; 85-90% photographed.

        Hours: daily 10-5. Fees: adults $4.00, students and
        seniors $1.50.

        Does not lend materials. Collection can be used by
        researchers.

                              * * *

BC99   VANCOUVER PUBLIC LIBRARY, FINE ARTS DIVISION

        Historical Photographs Section
        750 Burrard St.
        Vancouver, BC V62 1X5
        (604) 665-3388

        C. Middlemass, Visual Materials Librarian

        Offers slide kits on the history of CHINESE and
        JAPANESE immigration to British Columbia, including
        a history of Chinese settlement from 1858-1914,
        selections from the Philip Timms collection of
        photographs on the 1907 anti-Chinese riots on Pender
        Street, the F. Dundas Todd photographs of the fishing
        and farming industries and of the salmon cannery at
        Steveston (1913), and a history of the World War II

BC99   (Vancouver Public Library, Fine Arts Division)
cont.

expropriation and resettlement of British Columbia's
Japanese Canadians. Over 1,000 slides are of Chinese
Canadian, while 198 are of Japanese Canadian subjects.

Dates: 1850's-1940's.

Hours: M-Th 9:30-9:30; F-Sat 9:30-6:00; Sun (Fall,
Winter) 1-5.

Slide kits can be borrowed by registered library
patrons. Slides and prints of photographs in the
collection can be purchased. Access to original
material is limited on weekends and evenings.
Appointment unnecessary, but advance notice
appreciated.

* * *

BC100   PROVINCIAL ARCHIVES OF BRITISH COLUMBIA

655 Belleville St.
Victoria, BC V8V 1X4
(604) 387-1952

David Mattison, Librarian, Library and Maps Division
Staff: 42 permanent

The archives maintains black and white photographs
numbering in the hundreds of both CHINESE and JAPANESE
immigrant subjects, as well as dozens of documents
relating to Asian immigrant history and oral history
tapes of interviews conducted from the 1960's to the
present. It also has less than a dozen video tapes on
both Chinese and Japanese Canadian subjects.

Dates: 19th-20th c.

Hours: M-F 9-5. No admission fee; fees for copying.

Does not ordinarily lend materials, but the Visual
Records Division will loan to approved institutions
for exhibit purposes. No appointment necessary, but
researchers are advised to inquire about availability
of materials on-site since there may be delays in
retrieving materials stored outside the building.

* * *

BC101   HISTORIC YALE MUSEUM

31179 Douglas St.
Box 74
Yale, BC VOK 2SO
(604) 863-2324

British Columbia

BC101   (Historic Yale Museum)
cont.
        Beth Clare, Secretary/Treasurer
        Staff: 4 volunteer

        Articles in the museum represent the Gold Rush period
        in Yale and the building of the Canadian Pacific
        Railway. The museum, a private home built in 1868,
        maintains a small collection of CHINESE materials,
        including a basket with teapot and cups, 33 ceramic
        pieces, a meat saw, a shoulder yoke, cooking and
        eating utensils, brush pens, and an altar oil lamp.
        A monument in front of the museum honors Chinese
        railway workers.

        Dates: 1880's.

        Collection is catalogued.

        Hours: May-Sept, daily 9-5; Oct-Apr by appointment.
        Admission Fees: by donation.

        Does not lend materials. Collection can be used by
        researchers.

                                * * *

MB102   MANITOBA ARCHIVES BUILDING

        200 Vaughan Street
        Winnipeg, MB R3C 1T5
        (204) 945-4233

        Peter Bower, Provincial Archivist

        The archives has a few black and white photographs of
        CHINESE and JAPANESE Americans, as well as documents
        relating to the deportation of Japanese from British
        Columbia and their internment in Manitoba from 1942 to
        1946. Is currently receiving oral history tapes from
        the SOUTHEAST ASIAN Refugee Community Organization on
        the topic "Boat People and Walk People."

        Dates: early 1900's to present.

        Hours: M-F 8:30-5. Fees: None.

        Lends materials on microfilm.

                                * * *

ON103   MULTICULTURAL HISTORY SOCIETY OF ONTARIO

        Multicultural History Centre
        43 Queen's Park Crescent East
        Toronto, ON M5S 2C3
        (416) 979-2973

                          British Columbia-Manitoba-Ontario

ON103   (Multicultural History Society of Ontario)
cont.
       Contact: Archivist

       The society promotes research into the history of all
ethnocultural groups within the province of Ontario
and maintains manuscript and ethnic press publications
of institutional and individual materials, as well as
a significant collection of ethnic oral history tapes.
CHINESE materials include 122 hardcopy collections, 44
oral history tapes, 44 microfilm reels; FILIPINO
materials include 26 hardcopy collections and 25 oral
history tapes; JAPANESE materials include 51 hardcopy
collections, 94 oral history tapes, and 7 microfilm
reels; KOREAN materials include 87 hardcopy
collections, 103 oral history tapes and 7 microfilm
reels; and VIETNAMESE materials include 35 hardcopy
collections, 16 oral history tapes and 1 microfilm
reel.

       Dates: 1850's-present.

       Hours: M-F 9-5 pm. Fees for membership in society.

       Materials available to researchers. Sponsors
conferences and publishes proceedings, as well as the
series Ethnocultural Voices and Studies in Ethnic and
Immigration History and the semi-annual bulletin
Polyphony.

* * *

CHAPTER II

National Register and
Other Historical Sites

This chapter describes National Register and state register sites of Asian American significance. Some entries were abstracted from the 1976 edition of the National Register of Historic Places, complete through the end of 1974, while others derive from subsequent National Register files maintained by the Department of the Interior and from the California Historic Landmarks listing.

Cross-references to other entries are indicated where a direct overlap or correspondence of holdings exists, or where the entries are closely related.

AR104   ROHWER RELOCATION CENTER (NISEI CAMP)

Arkansas Highway 1
Rohwer, AR 71666

1942

Relocation camp which housed nearly 10,000 Americans
of JAPANESE descent in WWII when the government
carried out the policy of removing them from the West
Coast, an area thought to be strategically vulnerable.
Rohwer was the easternmost of 10 such camps. Concrete
foundations, a water tower, several buildings and
cemetery remain on the site.

Multiple public/private.

* * *

CA105   ANGEL ISLAND DETENTION CENTER

Angel Island, CA 94920

1910

On this island in the San Francisco Bay, CHINESE
immigrants, some of them family members of workers
already in the United States, were detained in
barracks while their papers for entry were being
processed. Detention on the island replaced the
practice of holding immigrants on the wharves or
on board ship when the restrictions of the Chinese
Exclusion Act of 1882 were instituted. The usual stay
was from two weeks to six months, but some detainees
were held in the barracks for two years. After
sometimes unreasonable and lengthy interrogations,
many would-be immigrants had to return to China.
The barracks and hospital building are still standing
on the site. One building now houses a museum in
which the poetry carved on the barracks' walls has
been reduplicated and other articles are held.

Cf. ANGEL ISLAND STATE PARK AND ANGEL ISLAND
    ASSOCIATION, CA25.

* * *

CA106   OLD AUBURN HISTORIC DISTRICT

Auburn, CA 95603

19th and early 20th c.

Auburn, established in 1849, was a former mining town
and commercial center between the northern and
southern mines of the Sierra Nevada. The old town
district, which includes numerous brick and frame

Arkansas-California

CA106   (Old Auburn Historic District)
cont.
          commercial structures, a county courthouse, and
          various dwellings, also had a CHINESE community and
          temple. The area was reconstructed after a fire in
          1855 and maintains its late 19th century appearance.
          The first Chinese railroad laborers were hired here by
          the Central Pacific Railroad to help complete the
          first transcontinental railroad. After considerable
          delay due to political opposition and lack of funding,
          the track reached Auburn on May 13, 1865. The
          government funds needed to complete the railroad only
          became available after the first 40 miles had been
          built, four miles east of Auburn.

          Multiple public/private.

                              * * *

CA107   CHINA CAMP

          SW shore of San Pablo Bay between San Pedro Pt. and
          San Rafael
          China Camp, CA 94901

          1860's

          The last surviving CHINESE shrimp fishing village in
          California, China Camp was established in the 1860's.
          The 1870 census lists 77 male shrimp fishermen living
          in 15 "dwelling units." Several structures remain,
          including a long narrow composite building used for
          drying shrimp, a red wood "shrimp shed," a wood-frame
          pier, and the existing camp store which was originally
          a shrimp grinding shed. The sea bed in the cove
          contains the hulls of three redwood vessels,
          presumably sampans. The San Francisco bay area once
          had thirty such villages, China camp being the
          earliest, largest and most productive. CANTONESE
          immigrants, who introduced commercial netting to catch
          bay shrimp, dried the shrimp on surrounding hillsides;
          then it was exported to China.

                              * * *

CA108   CHINESE CAMP

          Chinese Camp, CA 95309

          early 1850's

          Founded about 1849 by Englishmen employing CHINESE
          miners, the site became a headquarters for stage lines
          serving several California Chinese mining companies.
          Surface gold was discovered here as well in the nearby
          hills and flats. The first Chinese tong war was
          fought nearby between the Sam Yap and Yan Woo Tongs.

                                             California

CA108   (Chinese Camp)
cont.

Remaining from this period are a stone and brick post office built in 1854, which is still in use, and the St. Francis Xavier Catholic Church, built in 1855 and restored in 1949.

* * *

CA109   OLD HARMONY BORAX WORKS

Furnace Creek
Death Valley, CA 92328

1882

Borax was discovered in the marshes here by Aaron Winters. W. T. Coleman bought the claim from Winters and built the Old Harmony Borax Works. CHINESE workmen were hired to gather the ore. The processed borax was carried by 20-mule teams 165 miles to the nearest railroad.

* * *

CA110   DUTCH FLAT HISTORICAL DISTRICT

Main and Stockton Sts.
Dutch Flat, CA 95714

mid-late 19th c.

A gold rush town which was founded in 1851 by Joseph and Charles Dornback. With rich fields for hydraulic mining, by 1860 Dutch Flat had the largest voting population in Placer County and a large CHINESE population of about 2,000. It was here that the original subscription to build the first trans-continental railroad was made. The town has over 40 1-2 story buildings, many from the 1850's.

Multiple/private.

* * *

CA111   FONG WAH CEMETERY

Forest Highway 93
Forks of Salmon, Klamath National Forest, 96097

1850's

Formerly a burial place for CHINESE miners working in the Forks of Salmon vicinity, the cemetery is now abandoned. In accordance with common practice in the 1930's and 40's, the bodies were exhumed and the bones returned to China for final burial. The remains of

California

CA111   (Fong Wah Cemetery)
cont.
        walls built in the cemetery and various artifacts
        found in the graves have been maintained by the Forest
        Service.

                              * * *

CA112   WAKAMATSU TEA AND SILK FARM COLONY

        Gold Hill and Cold Springs Rds.
        Gold Hill, CA 95613

        1869

        JAPANESE immigrants, perhaps refugees escaping the new
        Japanese emperor of the restored Meiji, came to Gold
        Hill to establish a tea and silk farm under the
        direction of John Henry Schnell, a German soldier of
        fortune. Six immigrants arrived in June and sixteen
        others followed in the fall. They brought silk
        cocoons, young mulberry trees, teaplants and seeds,
        grape seedlings, bamboo roots, and other agricultural
        products from Japan. The children of Schnell and his
        Japanese wife were the first of Japanese ancestry to
        be born in the United States. The farm failed due to
        such problems as arid summer weather, diversion of
        water by upstream gold miners, and unsuitable soil.
        When the members of the colony dispersed, only the
        samurai Sakurai and the Schnell's nursemaid Okei
        remained. The grave of Okei is located on the knoll
        of a nearby hillside.

                              * * *

CA113   HANFORD TAOIST TEMPLE

        No. 10 China Alley
        Hanford, CA 93230

        1893

        Temple located on the commercial street of a CHINESE
        community of railroad and agricultural workers which
        was once the 2nd largest such community in the U.S.
        This 2 story brick structure with rear extension is
        among the oldest Taoist temples in the country. It has
        a rectangular flat roof, front veranda with chamfered
        posts and a 2nd floor balustrade. The center and end
        entrance is in a 3 bay facade with ornamental frieze
        and panels in corner pilasters. The original interior
        is maintained with furnishings, banners and costumes.

        Private, not accessible to the public.

                              * * *

                                                California

CA114   JENNY LIND

Jenny Lind, CA

1849

A placer mining town located on the north bank of the
Calaveras River. In 1864 half of the town's population
of 400 was CHINESE. The miners first dug along the
hillsides and then mined the river with dredgers.

* * *

CA115   LOCKE HISTORIC DISTRICT

Bounded by Locke Rd. Alley St. and Levee St.
Locke, CA

Early 20th c.

A community established by CHINESE laborers who were
hired to construct a vast levee system in the SW
Sacramento delta area when the 1915 fire forced them
to relocate. Buildings are 1-2 story frame commercial
and residential structures, many of which have 2nd
floor balconies and loading sheds (late 1880's) along
the top of the levee. Retains original appearance.

* * *

CA116   LOS ANGELES PLAZA HISTORIC DISTRICT

Los Angeles, CA 90012

ca 1800-20th c.

Established in 1815, the plaza is the site of the
founding of the City of Los Angeles and center of the
community during the city's 19th c. growth. Besides
the adobe Plaza Church (1818), the Avile Adobe (1818),
the Masonic Lodge (1858), and the Theater Mercedes
(1869), the main site includes the Victorian Garnier
Building (1890) which was built to accommodate CHINESE
businesses. Most buildings have vernacular and
European building elements. Partially restored.

Multiple public/private.

* * *

CA117   KOTANI-EN

W. of Los Gatos, Ravine Road
Los Gatos, CA 95030

1918

California

CA117   (Kotani-En)
cont.
         A classical JAPANESE residence surrounded by gardens
         in the tradition of formal landscape architecture,
         Kotani-En is one of the best examples of Japanese art
         and architecture in the U.S. San Francisco financier
         Max H. Cohn commissioned the Japanese architect
         Takashima to design and build the estate.
         Construction includes a 13th c.-style residence,
         a Buddhist temple, torii gates and a wall topped with
         black ceramic tile. The garden covering approximately
         1.5 acres includes a pond with imported carp,
         waterfalls, stone lanterns, rocks arranged in symbolic
         or mythological groupings, and over 200 species of
         plants.

         Private.

                              * * *

CA118   MANZANAR WAR RELOCATION CENTER

         6 mi. S. of Independence on CA 395

         1942

         First detention camp for JAPANESE immigrants during
         WWII. In accordance with Executive Order 9066 signed
         by Roosevelt in the Spring of 1942, Americans of
         Japanese descent were to be removed from Pacific
         coastal areas to inland camps. This camp, bounded by
         barbed wire and guard towers, confined 10,000 persons,
         the majority of whom were American citizens. The
         structures remaining are the auditorium, guardhouses,
         numerous foundations, and remains of a cemetery and
         gardens. The facility was closed in Nov. 1945.

         Municipal.

                              * * *

CA119   MARYSVILLE BOK KAI TEMPLE

         Yuba River Levee at D.St
         Marysville, CA 95901

         1880

         A CHINESE folk religious temple still in regular use
         honoring the water god Bok Kai, this one story brick
         rectangular structure combines mission and Chinese
         style elements. The temple has tile gabled roof
         sections with raised gable ends and a recessed front
         double door entrance, a full width front porch with
         turned columns and continuous hand-painted frieze,
         and side wings with separate entrances and porches.
         Regularly supplied with goods and materials by river

                                              California

CA119   (Marysville Bok Kai Temple)
cont.

boats via the Sacramento and Feather Rivers and by
stage coaches, Marysville's Chinatown became one of
the busiest and largest in the Northern Sacramento
Valley between 1850 and 1900 as miners and railroad
workers turned to farming, gardening, cooking,
laundering and other occupations. Marysville still
has a large Chinese community and sponsors a
celebration in the second month of the Chinese lunar
year in honor of Bok Kai, to which Chinese from other
areas of the United States come.

Private.

* * *

CA120   TEMPLE OF KUAN TI

45160 Albion St.
Mendocino, CA 95460

1854

One of the oldest of California's CHINESE temples
which has remained in use. Kuan Ti to whom the temple
is dedicated is the patron god of businessmen, as well
as a warlike figure in historical legend. He can be
recognized by his face, which is colored red. The
documented history of this temple begins in 1883.
Although many Chinese temples were built in the state,
most of them have been destroyed. This is the only
one from the early settlement period remaining on the
North Coast.

* * *

CA121   MORMON BAR

Mormon Bar, 2 mi. SE of Mariposa

1849

Members of the Mormon Battalion were the first to work
this mine, but they were soon replaced by other
miners. Thousands of CHINESE miners were able to mine
the area after others had moved to mine other
locations.

* * *

CA122   TULELAKE RELOCATION CENTER

Newell, CA

1942

CA122   (Tulelake Relocation Center)
cont.
         During World War II Tulelake was one of ten
         concentration camps used to incarcerate second
         generation Americans and first generation immigrants
         of JAPANESE ancestry who were living in the coastal
         areas of California. At Tulelake, although some
         groups organized resistance, they had little success,
         and as a result the restrictions at this camp were
         increased.

                              * * *

CA123   OROVILLE CHINESE TEMPLE

         1500 Broderick St.
         Oroville, CA 95965

         1863; 1968.

         A CHINESE local temple of various worships (Liet Sheng
         Kong), including elements of Taoism, Confucianism and
         Buddhism. The complex combines Western architectural
         and Chinese decorative elements. The one story Main
         Temple (1863) was built by Oroville's Chinese
         population with funds donated by the Ch'ing Emperor
         Quong She in celebration of his 29th reigning year.
         The complex also includes the two story Council Room
         and Moon Temple (1868-1870), as well as the recently
         constructed Tapestry Hall (1968), designed by the
         architect Philip Choy as a gallery to display the
         tapestries and other objects of historical
         significance. The adjoining Chinese courtyard garden
         and the grounds display plants and trees of Chinese
         origin. The temple continues to function as a museum,
         a community center, and a place of worship.

         Municipal

         Cf. CITY OF OROVILLE CHINESE TEMPLE, CA13

                              * * *

CA124   PARROTT GRANITE BLOCK

         California and Montgomery
         San Francisco, CA 94101

         1852

         The former site of a three-story building built by
         CHINESE immigrants and constructed by John Parrott, an
         importer and banker, with granite blocks from China,
         The 1906 earthquake and fire did little damage to the
         building. However, it was demolished in 1926.

                              * * *

CA125   BERINGER BROTHERS WINERY

St. Helena, CA 96042

1876

Established by Frederick and Jacob Beringer,
the winery is still in operation. The winery and
tunnels for aging the wine were built by CHINESE
laborers. The temperature in the tunnels averages 58
degrees year round.

* * *

CA126   AH LOUIS STORE

800 Palm St.
San Luis Obispo, CA 93401

1874

The first CHINESE store in the county, the Ah Louis
Store, established in 1874, served the local Chinese
immigrants. Between 1884 and 1894, Chinese laborers
built eight tunnels through the mountains of Cuesta.
Specializing in general merchandise and herbs, the Ah
Louis Store also served as a bank, a counting house,
and a post office.

* * *

CA127   WEAVERVILLE HISTORIC DISTRICT

Both sides of Main Street
Weaverville, CA 96093

mid-late 19th c.

A former goldmining town settled after 1849,
Weaverville had a large CHINESE community in the late
19th century. Located along main street and nearby
are 25 commercial, residential, public and religious
buildings of brick, frame and tamped earth
construction. The buildings along main street are 1-2
stories, often with false fronts or parapeted roofs
and many with verandas; several of the buildings
feature spiral iron stairs to 2nd floor verandas; also
remaining are a bandstand and an 1874 Chinese temple.
Furnishings and other articles are displayed in this
village-style temple still used as a place of worship.
Near the town is the site of an 1854 tong war.

Multiple public/private. SHP.

Cf. WEAVERVILLE JOSS HOUSE STATE HISTORIC PARK CA27

* * *

California

DC128   JAPANESE EMBASSY

2520 Mass. Ave. NW
Washington, DC 20008

1931-1932

The embassy's landscaping and outbuildings, including
a teahouse, are JAPANESE. Other buildings on the
grounds were designed by Western architects.

Private.

* * *

HI129   TONG WO SOCIETY HOUSE

Halawa, Hawaii, HI 96755

ca. 1886

This CHINESE society building was the temple and
meeting place for Hakka immigrants from Kwangtung who
were imported to work in the North Kohala sugar
industry established on the Island of Hawaii in the
1860's. Bachelors or married men with families left
in China, the founders gave their society the name of
"together in harmony." The activities of the
the Society increased when brides and families began
to come to North Kohala. The society house is a two-
story structure with a gabled roof. The building is
surrounded on both floors with open verandas which are
enclosed by a light balustrade with turned balusters.
Thin square posts which support each floor have
serpentine scroll sawn brackets. Other exterior
ornamental features include calligraphic plaques
framing the doorways and slight pedimental heads above
the windows. The second floor houses two small
altars, one honoring Kuan Ti, the Tong Wo Society's
patron saint, the other dedicated to Kuan Yin,
Goddess of Mercy. Besides the main building which is
still maintained, five other structures were
originally part of the society complex, including one
for entertainment, one for living quarters for the
elderly, and another in which members could die. A
preliminary burial was customary until the bones could
be removed by the society for proper re-burial in
native villages in China. Due to this practice, only
102 of the original 600 grave plots on the hillside
adjacent to the Tong Wo building remain filled. The
society was active from 1886 until its membership
dwindled in the 1940's as the workers and their
families moved from the plantation to urban areas.

Private.

* * *

HI130   KAWAILOA RYUSENJI TEMPLE

        N of Haleiwa at 179-A Kawailoa Drive
        Haleiwa, Oahu, HI 96813

        1914

        Located at the site of the Kawailoa Camp, this Soto
        Buddhist temple complex built for JAPANESE plantation
        workers includes a community hall, cookhouse,
        parsonage, caretaker's residence, bathhouse and a
        sheltered purification rock. The temple, consisting
        of a porch, a praying room and a columbarium, is a
        rectangular frame structure with a hip roof and end
        gables. The overhang at the gable ends is adorned
        with barge boards which have carved pendants at the
        ridge. The praying room is entered through a series
        of perimeter shoji partitions. Over the entrance to
        the praying room is a sculptured wooden panel carved
        by the shrine carpenter Kumazo Miyasaki. This fine
        example of immigrant craftsmanship depicts a huge
        dragon wading in a sea of rippling tides. The floor's
        surface is covered with finely woven mats. Silk and
        embroidered cloths hang over the support beams and the
        pillars before the shrine. A wooden bell-shaped
        container encases the Buddha figure on the shrine
        mantle. Over the shrine is a series of 48 hand
        sketched paintings set in low relief coffers. These
        samurai ink paintings depict the traditional motifs
        of landscapes, Zen and folktale figures, flowers,
        trees, animals and birds. The temple served the
        immigrant community by holding funeral and memorial
        services and organizing religious festivals, including
        the New Year celebration with its parties and mochi
        (rice cake) pounding. Kawailoa became famous for its
        rice cakes which were sold by the congregation for
        money-making purposes.

        Private.

                            * * *

HI131   CHEE YING SOCIETY HOUSE

        Route 24, Kukuihaele Road
        Honokaa, Hawaii, HI

        1907

        One of the few remaining CHINESE society houses in
        Hawaii, this building was the mainstay of the
        religious and cultural life of Chinese workers who
        belonged to the Hung Men Society. These workers from
        Kwangtung, Fukien and Shantung were employed by the
        Honokaa Sugar Plantation. The society house, a square
        two-story frame structure with a two-story porch
        divided into five equal bays, has a gable roof

HI131   (Chee Ying Society House)
cont.
         surrounded at the eaveline by a hip roof. The first
         floor holds the community room while the second floor
         is a temple. Surrounding the panel doors leading to
         both sections of the building are calligraphic
         plaques: those around the first floor doors are
         painted while the characters surrounding the doors to
         the temple are jigsawn. At the altar is the remains
         of a Kuan Ti painting flanked by papers with Chinese
         characters. On the society grounds are also a wood
         frame cook house, the remains of a house probably used
         to house the elderly and sick, a pork cooker and two
         cemeteries, one of which still has headstones with
         visible Chinese calligraphy. The festivals known to
         have been celebrated at the house were the Kuan Ti
         Festival, the Chinese New Year, and the April Ching
         Ming Festival.

         Private.

                           * * *

HI132   CHINATOWN HISTORIC DISTRICT

         Bounded roughly by Beretania St. on the NE, Nuuanu
         Stream on the N, Nuuanu Ave. on the SE and Honolulu
         Harbor
         Honolulu, Oahu, HI 96815

         ca. 1810

         A cultural and commercial district now occupied not
         only by ethnic CHINESE, but JAPANESE, HAWAIIAN,
         KOREAN, PHILIPPINE and VIETNAMESE immigrant groups.
         Located close to the harbor, this area early became an
         area focused on business and trade. Most structures
         are two- or three-story buildings made of brick, cut
         blue stone, frame, concrete and hollow tile with
         eclectic and pseudo-oriental elements. These date
         primarily from the early 20th c. due to destructive
         fires in 1886 and 1900. Places of special historic
         and cultural interest in Chinatown include herb shops,
         a print shop and the Kuan Yin temple. Located on N.
         Beretania is the recently constructed Chinese Cultural
         Plaza, housing restaurants, shops and offices, with an
         adjoining market. The central plaza is used for
         various cultural and educational activities.

         Tours of Chinatown are offered by the Chinese Chamber
         of Commerce (808 533-3181) and by the Hawaii Heritage
         Center (808 521-2749).

         Multiple Private/Public

                           * * *

HI133   WALKER RESIDENCE

        2616 Pali Highway
        Honolulu, Oahu, HI 96815

        1905

        The residence of H. Alexander Walker, this estate
        probably has Hawaii's oldest formal JAPANESE
        garden.   The residence itself is a two-story
        irregularly shaped frame house.

        Private.

                            * * *

HI134   GROVE FARM

        On HI 501 about 1 mi. SE of Lihue
        Lihue, Kauai, HI 96766

        ca. 1854

        This sugar plantation where large numbers of JAPANESE,
        as well as CHINESE, PHILIPPINE and PORTUGUESE,
        contract labourers worked is the only plantation
        homestead left in Hawaii.   The remarkable state of
        preservation of buildings and grounds demonstrate the
        architectural heritage of Hawaii.   Remaining in the
        complex are numerous single-story frame buildings,
        including the original residence, guest cottage,
        Wilcox cottage, office building, a teahouse built in
        1898 by a Japanese household employee named Suehiro,
        and the Kaipu Camp outbuildings occupied by the
        plantation workers.   The farm was built under the
        direction of George N. Wilcox, one of the state's most
        prominent and influential citizens.

        Private.

                            * * *

HI135   LIHUE HONGWANJI MISSION

        N of Lihue at Kapaia, Highway 56
        Lihue, Kauai, HI 96766

        1901

        The oldest JAPANESE Buddhist Mission still in
        existence on Kauai.   Now located among several other
        buildings related to the mission, the original temple
        was built by Japanese laborers brought to Hawaii
        specifically for this purpose.   It is a single-story
        wood frame structure with a hip roof and small gable
        ends.   The windows are rectilinear, double hung with
        small curved pediments in the form of Japanese Genkon

HI135   (Lihue Hongwanji Mission)
cont.
         entry roofs. The gabled entry roof is supported by
         two square wooden columns on the raised front entry
         porch. The building is entered through sliding wood
         frame glass doors that open the full width of the
         porch. A large altar faces the entry.

         Private.

                              * * *

HI136   MAUI JINSHA MISSION

         472 Lipo Street
         Wailuku, Maui, HI 96793

         1915

         One of the few remaining older JAPANESE Shinto shrines
         in Hawaii, this mission is a good example of the
         Nagata style. Construction was begun under Head
         Carpenter Seichi Tomokiyo and completed by Master
         Carpenter Ichitaro Takata, both from Japan. The
         shrine area is entered through a torii gate, and two
         entrance shrines flank the paved walk leading to the
         main shrine. The mission building, surrounded by
         neatly landscaped open lawns and trees, is a
         rectangular wooden structure raised on posts in a
         series of platforms and steps rising first to the
         larger temple area and then up to the smaller shrine
         in the rear. The hip roof is covered with shingles
         and has an ornamental ridgepole with chigi (V-shaped
         projections) above the ridge. An open veranda
         stretches across the front while narrow veranda areas
         are located at the two sides of the smaller shrine.
         Exposed beams and rafters in a natural wood finish are
         carved and painted. Lintels, brackets, and bargeboard
         pieces are also carved. The large panel which hangs
         over the entrance to the shrine's main hall depicts
         "The Thousand Horses," the 1,000 people who each gave
         a dollar toward building the shrine.

         Private.

                              * * *

HI137   WAKAMIYA INARI SHRINE

         Waipahu Cultural Garden
         near Waipahu, Oahu, HI 96797

         1914, 1918

         A JAPANESE Shinto shrine of the Inari sect, this
         is the only example of this Shinto sect's traditional
         shrine architecture on Oahu. It is a rectangular

                                                      Hawaii

HI137   (Wakamiya Inari Shrine)
cont.

frame building which is painted red and has a shake
shingled _irimoya_ (hipped and gabled) roof with
overhanging eaves, exposed rafters, and an ornamental
ridgepole with _chigi_ (V-shaped projections). A set of
wood steps with a simple balustrade leads up to the
shrine. A balustraded porch wraps around the front
and two sides of the sanctuary. Sliding doors enclose
the sanctuary which contains an elevated central
altar. The floor of the sanctuary is covered with
rice mats. The shrine has been moved from its former
locations first in the Kakaako section of Honolulu and
then on King Street. In its present location in the
Waipahu Cultural Garden, the shrine's original front
garden space containing traditional stone statuary and
a _torii_ gateway are maintained.

Private.

* * *

NY138   NEW YORK CHINATOWN

Bounded by Baxter St. on the W, Park Row and the
Bowery on the S and E and Canal Street on the N
New York, NY 10013

The first CHINESE immigrants began to congregate on
Mott, Doyer and Pell Streets in the 1850's and 60's,
but the Chinese Exclusion Act of 1882 halted the
growth of the area until 1942. Since then, the area
has continued to grow as a center for ethnic foods and
services for the Chinese community in the greater New
York area. Places of historic or cultural interest
include the statue of Confucius in Confucius Plaza at
Division and Bowery, the Manhattan Savings Bank at
Catherine and Bowery with its curved tile roof and
figured detail, the Eastern States Buddhist Temple of
America at 64 Mott Street, the Kuan Yin Buddhist
Temple at 16 Pell Street, and a _pai-lou_ (memorial
gate) at Chatham Square which was constructed in
memory of Chinese American soldiers who fought in the
United States forces during WW II. The Chinese
lettering on the gate is the work of Yu You-ren,
a famous 20th century calligrapher.

Art tours are sponsored by the Chinese American Arts
Council (212/431-9740). Historical tours are
conducted by the New York Chinatown History Project
Center (212/619-4785).

Cf. NEW YORK CHINATOWN HISTORY PROJECT, NY64
    ASIAN AMERICAN FESTIVAL, NY176
    CHINATOWN SUMMER CULTURAL FESTIVAL, NY177

* * *

OR139   SAMUEL ELMORE CANNERY

        On the waterfront, at the foot of Flavel St.
        Astoria, OR 97103

        1881

        The country's oldest continuously operated salmon
        cannery. CHINESE laborers worked here during the
        early 1900's and were housed in the two-story
        bunkhouse. The cannery complex also includes the
        original main canning and storage buildings.

        Private.

        National Historic Landmark

                              * * *

OR140   KAM WAH CHUNG COMPANY BUILDING

        Canton St.
        John Day City Park
        John Day, OR 97845

        ca. 1866

        A trading center, doctor's office and social center
        for a CHINESE immigrant mining community of over
        1,000. The building is a stone (large round-cut
        blocks) structure, with one to one and a half story
        sections, small windows and doors, outside stairs to
        frame the second floor with horizontal siding;
        original furnishings and supplies intact. Museum.

        Municipal.

        Cf. KAM WAH CHUNG AND CO. MUSEUM, OR68
            KAM WAH CHUNG DAYS, OR180

                              * * *

UT141   TOPAZ WAR RELOCATION CENTER SITE

        16 mi. NW of Delta
        Delta, UT

        1942-1943

        One of ten camps built to house JAPANESE immigrants
        inland during World War II when the United States
        administration determined that their presence in
        coastal areas put the nation at risk. Over 8,000
        first, second and third generation Japanese immigrants
        were housed at this camp. The foundations of camp
        buildings and the street system remain of the original
        19,000 acre area which included 42 blocks with 628

UT141   (Topaz War Relocation Center Site)
cont.

buildings, 12 one-story barracks buildings, each
with six dormitory rooms, a central dining hall, a
recreational hall and administration buildings. This
detention area was opened on Sept. 11, 1942 and closed
on Oct. 31, 1945.

Private.

* * *

WA142   CHINESE SOUTHERN BAPTIST MISSION CHURCH

925 S. King Street
Seattle, WA 98104

1922

This CHINESE Baptist mission begun in 1896 in Seattle
is representative of Christian missions established on
the West Coast for the immigrant community in the late
1800's. Constructed in 1922 to replace an original
frame structure, the mission church was sold in 1976
and used as a warehouse. In 1987, the building was
re-purchased by the mission, and it now serves as a
multi-culture center for the Chinese Southern
Baptist Mission, the FILIPINO Baptist Fellowship and
the Metropolitan Baptist Chapel. Traditionally,
pastors in the church are Christians of Chinese
descent.

* * *

WA143   NIPPON KAN OR ASTOR HOTEL

622 South Washington Street
Seattle, WA 98104

1909

This large three and a half story brick building, both
theater and hotel, was an important entertainment and
meeting place for the JAPANESE immigrants in Seattle's
Nihonmachi or Japantown, an area once occupying an
area of 27 city blocks with a population of over 6,000
before the depression and the WW II relocation.
To avoid the discriminatory laws which denied land
ownership to non-citizens, a group of Japanese
American businessmen used the name of a Caucasian
"front man" to get permission to build the hall and
hotel. Storefronts occupy most of the groundfloor
exterior. The entrance to the hotel is to the north
of the centermost east-facing store front, which
contains the theater entrance. The upper floor
hotel area containing small 10 feet square rooms
arranged around two light wells was the temporary

WA143   (Nippon Kan or Astor Hotel)
cont.

residence of Japanese workers who would be hired out
as miners, railroad builders, migrant farmers, and
cannery and sawmill workers. The flat-floor theater
is a rectangular space 60 by 80 feet with a proscenium
stage built directly on the floor. At the rear of the
stage is a curtain which contains Japanese characters,
some of which advertise local businesses. A four-feet
wide notch stage-right reveals that a traditional
Japanese theater feature, the runway or hanamichi,
once extended from the stage. Names of Japanese
Americans dating to 1918 cover the rear of the
proscenium walls. Amateur entertainment prevailed in
the theater. For the Issei or first generation,
ancient Japanese plays and shamisen, shakuhachi and
classical odori performances were presented, but
amateur harmonica players, vocalists, violinists,
pianists and comedians also performed in the theater.

Private.

* * *

BC144   VANCOUVER CHINATOWN

West Pender between Carrall and Gore
Vancouver, BC V6J 3J9

1880

Vancouver has the second largest Chinatown in North
America. Since the 1880's, West Pender (originally
DuPont St.) has been the locus of CHINESE merchants,
grocers, tea merchants and launderers. Many of the
original dwellings were wooden buildings built with
piling in the marshes at the end of False Creek. As
a result of a movement led by young professionals to
protect the community, residents were given government
loans to upgrade their houses. In all, 200 private
houses were renovated. Of special historical interest
is a building on the northwest corner of Pender and
Carrall where Dr. Sun Yat Sen, the father of the
Chinese Revolution, lived. A classical Ming Dynasty
garden was recently constructed in his honor by
artisans brought to Vancouver from China. Many of the
natural and man-made materials were imported from
Suzhou, China's garden city.

Information and tours are available through the
Vancouver Chinese Cultural Centre, 50 East Pender St.

* * *

CHAPTER III

Festivals

The festival entries in this section derive from a questionnaire mailed to various civic, ethnic and cultural associations, from information in festival notices, and from Chamber of Commerce and newspaper files. The dates for many annual festivals are variable; therefore, in many cases only approximate dates are provided.

The festivals listed are celebrations which are generally organized by members of ethnic secular and religious organizations, but in which all Americans may participate as observers and even sometimes as performers. That is, not only do members of the ethnic group share with each other demonstrations of their current traditional and modern cultural achievements, but they also present and interpret their cultural heritage for the public at large. Many of the ethnic festivals which are celebrated mainly in the family are not listed here.

Major festivals in metropolitan areas attract the greatest attention, and, because they are multi-sponsored, are able to present a great variety of events. These are the festivals best represented in this directory; however, it should be noted that such festivals as the Chinese New Year and the Japanese Obon Festival are also celebrated with great élan in smaller communities not represented here. The following introduction explains briefly the origins and observances of some of these major festivals celebrated in the United States and Canada.

Festivals Introduction

One of the most widely celebrated Asian ethnic festivals
in North America is the Chinese New Year. With a long
tradition of celebration by Chinese Americans and Chinese
Canadians, a great variety of events, both traditional
Chinese and American, are usually arranged by several
sponsoring groups. The celebration lasts fifteen days
beginning at midnight on the first day of the first lunar
month each year. Since the lunar calendar month is 29 1/2
days long and special lunar calculations must be made to
determine the New Year date for each separate year, the
Chinese New Year may occur anytime from mid-January to
mid-to-late February on the solar Gregorian calendar. As
calculated in San Francisco's Chinatown for the San Francisco
Convention and Visitors' Bureau, the dates for the festival
until the year 2000 are as follows: Jan. 27, 1990; Feb. 15,
1991; Feb. 4, 1992; Jan. 23, 1993; Feb. 10, 1994; Jan. 31,
1995; Feb. 19, 1996; Feb. 7, 1997; Jan. 28, 1998; Feb. 16,
1999; and Feb. 5, 2000.

The first day, or in some cases several days, of the
Chinese New Year is usually one of family observances with
offerings to ancestors, the setting off of firecrackers, the
distribution of red envelopes containing money to children,
and visits to friends and relatives. On following days, a
major parade with floats and lion dancers is held, special
arts and crafts are displayed or demonstrated, and musical
performances are presented. The traditional lion dances play
an important role in most celebrations of the Chinese New
Year. The lion, with a twelve foot long body and an ornately
decorated papier mâché and bamboo head, is given a welcome at
local businesses which offer him money wrapped in red paper.
The owners hope that in return their businesses will prosper
during the coming year. All during the festival days,
special foods are available, including chiao-tzu, dumplings
with various fillings, and nien-kao, a glutinous rice cake
symbolizing family unity. During the New Year celebration in
San Francisco, Ms. Chinatown USA is chosen from the more than
fifteen candidates selected in contests previously held in
Chinese communities all around the country. The New Year
period comes to a close on the fifteenth of the month with
the Lantern Festival when there are parades or displays of
decorative lanterns.

The Japanese Lunar New Year or Setsebun is now largely
celebrated by banquets and family dinners. It is the Cherry
Blossom Festival held later in the spring that has become the
major showcase for the arts and crafts of Japanese culture in
several metropolitan areas, including Honolulu, San
Francisco, and Toronto. Japanese Americans from nearby areas
and Japanese performers and visitors journey to these cities
to join local Japanese Americans in parades, performances,
and demonstrations. So, while in Japan people may go to the
mountains to view the first spring blossoms, make pilgrimages
to famous historical places and temples and eat and drink in
the outdoors with friends, North American Japanese share
their cultural heritage with interested observers in American
and Canadian urban communities.

Adhering closely to Japanese tradition are the Obon Festival services and dances. The Obon Festival is said to have originated in a Buddhist tradition commemorating the rescue from hell of the mother of Maudgalyayana, one of Buddha's disciples. Maudgalyayana's mother was able to achieve nirvana because her son was so compassionate and charitable in his actions. The religious legend tells that the mother danced from joy, as did others, who joined in the celebration to express their gratitude for this rewarding of good deeds with a deliverance from hell (de Francis, 44-45). While related to a Hindu ceremony of releasing souls from hell, this Buddhist festival as celebrated by Japanese may also have adopted observances originating in Japan.

In North American Japanese communities, the Bon season lasts from June until August, being celebrated on different weekends in several of the temples in one area. Dances and temple ceremonies mark this occasion. In preparation, a wooden tower is built in the center of the dancing area. It is then decorated with colorful lanterns and decorations, and concentric circles are painted around it. During the festival, the dancers, some wearing traditional summer kimonos, dance around the tower to a drum and live or taped music, which varies from traditional folk to modern. Bon dancers may include entire families and even non-Japanese friends. Japanese foods are served. As Luana Fukutomi notes from personal experience in "The Bon Dance Festival in Rural Hawaii," where there are many Japanese Buddhist temples, dances are held on different weekends at different temples so people may enjoy participating in the festivities at several temples in one year and visiting with old friends. While Bon dances are open to the public, usually the temple services which honor deceased members are not. In Hawaii these services culminate with lantern boats being carried to the water's edge and launched out to sea with offerings of flowers and food.

Other yearly festivals celebrated by the ethnic community have fewer non-ethnic participants or observers. Such Chinese festivals include the fall Chinese Moon Festival and the spring Ching Ming and Dragon Boat Festivals, when special foods are eaten and rituals are sometimes performed. Among the Japanese festivals of this kind are the Girls' and Boys' Days, when special foods are prepared, department stores have special displays, and families and friends gather to celebrate much in the traditional manner. It should be noted that the arts and crafts which accompany these festivals form the major component of festival arts collections listed in the first section of this directory.

Most Korean and Filipino immigrants to North America are Christians and in general celebrate Christian holidays. However, in the Koreatowns of Los Angeles and Chicago, the cities with the largest Korean population, an ethnic festival is held annually or biannually. At these festivals Korean arts are displayed, and there is a parade, as well as contests and games.

For Filipino immigrants to North America, Christmas remains the most celebrated holiday. Aside from the major Saints' Day observances at Catholic Churches, in Filipino American parishes made up of people from a particular region or city in the Philippines, local religious celebrations are

also maintained. Some Filipino Americans in Los Angeles
celebrate Ati-Atihan, for instance, a mid-January festival.
Other celebrations derive from special local religious
holidays in Balayan, Batangas and Apalit, Pampanga, both
observed in June mainly by immigrants from those areas. More
generally observed in North America is Santacruzan which is
celebrated the first week in May. Marked in the Philippines
by elaborate floral processions, it is often celebrated by
immigrant communities in parish churches. Filipino Americans
also commemorate Philippine Independence Day with a round of
special dances, dinners, parades, and displays. In San
Francisco this national celebration lasts an entire week.
     Southeast Asians, many of them recent refugees or
immigrants from Vietnam, Cambodia, Indonesia, and Laos, are
also joining together in their own celebrations as they begin
to congregate in particular geographical areas. For
instance, in Merced, California, Hmong, Mien, and Laotian
people perform their traditional dances at the Festival of
Cultures held in October. The Hmong celebrate New Years,
though, largely among themselves the last of December with
traditional games and special foods. In urban areas, such as
New York, Los Angeles, Houston, and Seattle, Southeast Asians
are invited by the sponsoring agencies, primarily ethnic
Chinese, to participate in Pan Asian or other Asian cultural
festivals. It should also be noted that some of the recent
immigrants from Southeast Asia are of Chinese descent and
participate in the already established Chinese festivals in
the United States and Canada.

References

        Chang, Toy Len. Chinese Festivals the Hawaiian Way.
Honolulu: Toy Len Chang, 1983.

        De Francis, John. Things Japanese in Hawaii.
Honolulu: U of Hawaii P, 1973.

        Fukutomi, Luana. "The Bon Dance Festival in Rural
Hawaii." Bloomington, IN: Indiana University Folklore
Archives, 1974.

        Haga, Hideo. Japanese Folk Festivals, Illustrated.
Trans. Fanny Hagin Mayer. Tokyo: Miura Printing, 1970.

        Werner, E. T. C. A Dictionary of Chinese Mythology.
New York: Julian, 1969.

AZ145 MATSURI FESTIVAL

Heritage Square
7th St. and Monroe, Phoenix

City of Phoenix Parks, Recreation and Library Dept.
125 E. Washington St.
Phoenix, AZ 85001
(602) 262-6861

Phoenix's Sister City in Himeji, Japan joins with
local JAPANESE American groups and other Phoenix
citizens in presenting folk craft displays,
traditional processions, demonstrations of martial
arts, flower arranging and the tea ceremony, as well
as in performances of folk singing, dancing and
drumming. Modern professional entertainment is
provided by guest artists from Japan, as well as by
Japanese American artists. Photographs of scenes of
Japan are on exhibit. Local Japanese restaurants run
food booths.

Date: late Feb.

* * *

CA146 KOREAN FESTIVAL

Koreatown, Olympic Blv., Vermont Ave. to Western Ave.
Los Angeles

Gene Kim, Founder and Honorary Chairman
Koreatown Development Association
981 S. Western Ave., #200B
Los Angeles, CA 90006
(213) 730-1495 or 730-1527

Ethnic KOREAN events held in several locations in
Koreatown include a traditional marketplace, live
vocal performances, dances, a traditional costume
show, a children's art exhibition, craft and martial
arts displays, a carnival, a songfest, and several
contests, including a kite contest, Oriental chess
matches, a calligraphy contest, a photography contest,
and a beauty contest. A parade is held toward the end
of the festival in which the new Miss Junior Korea,
chosen in the beauty contest, is presented with her
court.

Dates: mid-Sept for one week.

Koreatown archival materials are available at the
Univ. of Southern California Library.

* * *

CA147 NISEI WEEK

Little Tokyo, San Pedro St.
Los Angeles

Nisei Week Festival Office
244 S. San Pedro St., Room 501
Los Angeles, CA 90012
(213) 687-7193

A JAPANESE festival which begins with the Shinto
ritual of dedication and purification and the opening
of Sakadaru (the sake barrel). The celebration
includes a grand parade of dancers in kimono, taiko
drummers, floats, marching bands and celebrities and a
5-km run through the streets of Little Tokyo. Bonsai,
ikebana (flower arrangement), shodo (calligraphy),
dolls, and swords are displayed, and demonstations of
the tea ceremony are given. The activities culminate
in the middle of the month with a carnival and the
Ondo Street Dance with drummers and hundreds of
dancers costumed in the summer cotton Yukata kimono.

Date: in Aug, for ten days.

Audience participation in dance is welcomed.

* * *

CA148 CHERRY BLOSSOM FESTIVAL (SAKURA MATSURI)

Japantown, Post and Buchanan Streets
San Francisco

San Francisco Convention and Visitors' Bureau
201 Third Street
San Francisco, CA 94103
(415) 974-6900

A JAPANESE celebration of spring with a parade,
martial arts demonstrations, ethnic dancing, flower
arranging, tea ceremonies, taiko drums, koto music,
and sumo wrestling matches. Films on Japan and
special exhibits are shown. Japanese foods are sold
at a bazaar. A special event is the 5-mile Cherry
Blossom Run. Japanese American groups from other
areas of California and the West Coast join in the
celebration.

Dates: two weekends in mid- and late Apr.

Most events are free.

* * *

CA149   CHINESE NEW YEAR

Chinatown, bounded by Stockton, Bush, Broadway and
Kearny Streets, San Francisco

San Francisco Convention and Visitor's Bureau
201 Third Street
San Francisco, CA 94103
(415) 974-6900

CHINESE Lunar New Year is celebrated with outdoor
parades, plays, a Ms. Chinatown USA contest, and New
Year walks explaining special window displays led by
docents from the Chinese Culture Foundation. Displays
and events also include floral decorations, festival
foods, sports events, art exhibits, photo exhibitions,
cooking and martial arts demonstrations, folk and
classical music and dance performances, lion dancing,
fashion shows, and the Asian Week/YMCA Chinatown Run,
an 8 km race from Chinatown YMCA, at 855 Sacramento
St., through Chinatown and North Beach and along the
Embarcadero.

Dates: Lunar New Year (see dates for coming years in
       Festivals introduction)

The Chinese Historical Society of America, 17 Adler
Place off 1140 Grant Ave. can provide information
about past festivals and customs associated with the
celebration of the Chinese New Year.

Cf. CHINESE HISTORICAL SOCIETY OF AMERICA, CA20.

* * *

CA150   PHILIPPINE AMERICAN CULTURAL WEEK AND FIESTA

Union Square, San Francisco

Dalisay Bocobo-Balunsat
1437 19th Ave.
San Francisco, CA 94122
(415) 665-5763

Celebrations and events surrounding PHILIPPINE
Independence Day. Two days of Fiesta events at Union
Square include a beauty pagaent parade of contestants
selected from the Northern California Filipino
American organizations, processions of religious clubs
and groups, performances by local Filipino singers
and traditional dancers, as well as by bands and
dancers from the Philippines. Arts and crafts,
traditional games and a mini-Philippine village are
displayed. Food is sold by local Filipino
restaurants. Other events earlier in the week-long
round of festivities include the traditional town
fiesta celebration of Capoocan, Leyte held by the

California

CA150   (Philippine American Cultural Week and Fiesta)
cont.
        Association of the Holy Child Sto. Nino of Capoocan,
        Leyte: after a traditional mass is observed at St.
        Joseph's Church, there is a dinner and dance. Picnics
        and church celebrations, as well as a grand dinner and
        ball also a part of the Independence celebrations.

        Dates: a week in mid-June (Fiesta days 12-13).

                              * * *

CA151   CHINESE NEW YEAR

        Civic Auditorium, Stockton

        San Joaquin Convention and Visitors Bureau
        Stockton, CA 95213
        (209) 466-1416

        The CHINESE Lunar New Year is celebrated by the
        community with performances and displays by local and
        guest Chinese artists. The program includes folk
        dance performances, acupuncture and kung-fu
        demonstrations, a traditional costume show, an art
        exhibit and puppet show.

        Dates: Lunar New Year (see dates for coming years in
               Festivals introduction).

                              * * *

CA152   FILIPINO BARRIO FESTIVAL

        Civic Auditorium, Stockton

        San Joaquin Convention and Visitor's Bureau
        Stockton, CA 95213
        Contact: (209) 466-1416

        Traditional dance and FILIPINO cultural programs, food
        and entertainment by local Filipino Americans and
        guest performers.

        Date: in Aug.

                              * * *

DC153   ASIAN PACIFIC AMERICAN HERITAGE COUNCIL FESTIVAL

        Washington Monument Grounds, Washington, DC

        Organization of Chinese Americans, Northern Virgina,
        P.O. Box 592
        Merrifield, VA 22116
        (703) 241-8759

                              California-District of Columbia

DC153   (Asian Pacific American Heritage Council Festival)
cont.
          All Asian Pacific ethnic groups participate in this
          festival. The Northern Virginia Chapter of the
          Organization of CHINESE Americans has participated
          with sales of papercuts and other craft displays.

          Dates: 1st wk. in May (Asian Pacific American Heritage
                 Festival Week).

                              * * *

DC154   BURMESE WATER FESTIVAL

          in DC area park

          Betty Tin, Secretary
          Burmese Association of the Capital Area
          14010 Crest Hill Lane
          Silver Spring, MD 20904
          (301) 384-0691

          The BURMESE New Year, ordinarily around April 15, is
          celebrated in the Washington area on Memorial Day
          weekend. This Water Festival is celebrated by
          participants from all areas of the Eastern seaboard.
          At the celebration, the participants throw water on
          one another as a symbol of cleansing. The festival is
          also celebrated with ethnic craft displays, secular
          dances, and traditional and modern performances, as
          well as a gigantic potluck dinner, mainly of Burmese
          dishes provided by the Washington area residents.

          Date: Memorial Day weekend.

          Bringing a change of clothing is recommended.
          Videotapes and historical materials on past festival
          celebrations are available in a personal collection
          which is accessible through special arrangement.

                              * * *

DC155   CHINESE COMMUNITY CHURCH ANNUAL SPRING FESTIVAL

          Chinese Community Church
          1011 L. St. NW
          Washington, DC 20001
          (202) 232-9495

          CHINESE arts and crafts are displayed and performances
          of music and folk dancing and marital arts are given.
          Chinese KOREAN, JAPANESE and VIETNAMESE food provided.

          Dates: Lunar New Year (see dates for coming years in
                 Festivals introduction).

                              * * *

                                           District of Columbia

DC156   CHINESE NEW YEAR

Chinese Cultural Center
H and I Streets, NW, between Sixth and 11th Sts.
Washington, DC 20001
(202) 223-3494

CHINESE New Year is celebrated at the center with
firecrackers, dragon dances and special foods.

Dates: Lunar New Year (see dates for coming years in
       Festivals introduction).

* * *

DC157   SPRING FESTIVAL AND BAZAAR

Mt. Vernon College

Japan-America Society of Washington
1302 18th St. NW
Washington, DC 20036
(202) 223-1772

A JAPANESE ethnic festival with demonstrations of
martial arts, koto concerts, and arts and crafts
displays and sales, including ikebana and bonsai;
also has food booths and sales of old books and
prints.

Dates: in Apr.

* * *

DC158   SPRING FLOWER FESTIVAL

United States National Arboretum or
United States Botanic Garden, Washington, DC

Mrs. Duane E. Erickson, President
Ikebana International, Chapter #1
P.O. Box 9663
Washington, DC 20016-9663
(301) 933-5928

The Spring Flower Festival held annually displays
JAPANESE flower arrangements and some bonsai. Live
demonstrations are given by teachers of various
schools of ikebana. Sometimes, kimono shows and
koto performances are also presented.

Dates: last of Apr-first of May, for one week.

Brochures of past festivals and other archival
materials are available.

* * *

District of Columbia

HI159   INTERNATIONAL FESTIVAL OF THE PACIFIC

Hilo, Hawaii

Japanese Chamber of Commerce
476A Hinano
Hilo, Hawaii, HI 96720
(808) 961-6123

A multicultural festival with costumes and dances of
CHINESE, JAPANESE, KOREAN, FILIPINO and other ethnic
groups of Hawaii. The events may be centered around a
ship in port at Hilo. Ethnic foods are sold.

Dates: mid-summer.

* * *

HI160   BON ODORI AND FLOATING LANTERN FESTIVAL

Jodo Mission, Haleiwa on the North Shore

Jodo Mission
1429 Makiki St.
Honolulu, Oahu, HI 96814

On all islands of Hawaii the JAPANESE Bon Festival is
celebrated with religious services, folk dancing,
chanting, singing and drumming at Buddhist temples
(see Festivals introduction). The Jodo Mission, in
particular, also observes the Floating Lantern
Festival. Following a service during which <u>sutras</u> are
chanted, food and flower offerings, along with the
names of the dead, are placed on a boat called the
Mother Boat. Smaller lantern boats with candles in
them accompany the Mother Boat as it is launched out
to sea.

Dates: at the Jodo Mission Fri-Sat from dusk to
midnight at the full moon in July or Aug; Bon
dancing nights at different temples on several
weekends in July and August.

Although the Jodo Mission's services are by invitation
only, visitors can participate in the dances and
observe the floating lanterns.

* * *

HI161   BOYS' DAY

Department stores, offices and homes in Honolulu and
throughout Hawaii

On this JAPANESE ethnic holiday, male dolls which
represent courtiers, warriors, knights, and martial
arts figures, with accessory weapons and armor, are

Hawaii

HI161   (Boys' Day)
cont.

given as gifts and appear in cultural displays. Mochi
cakes shaped like samurai helmuts are sold in
bakeries. Koi-nobori, carp streamers made of paper
or cloth up to twenty feet in length, are flown.

Date: May 5.

* * *

HI162   BUDDHA DAY (BODHI DAY) OR HANA MATSURI

At Waikiki Shell, Kapiolani Park and at various
temples throughout Hawaii

Hawaiian Buddhist Council
1727 Pali Highway
Honolulu, Oahu, HI 96813
(808) 538-3805

Flower festival pageants at JAPANESE temples statewide
commemorate the birth of Shakamuni Buddha. Flowers
cover the shrine in which the infant Buddha is
placed. After the services, during which Buddhist
hymns are sung and sutras chanted, sweet tea is poured
upon the Buddha by worshippers. Children from
various temples participate in public programs in
honor of the Buddha. A potluck dinner may follow.

Date: Sunday nearest Apr 8 (Apr 8 is a state holiday).

* * *

HI163   CHERRY BLOSSOM FESTIVAL

Honolulu, Oahu

Gerald Oyasato
Honolulu Japanese Junior Chamber of Commerce
2454 South Beretania Street
Honolulu, Oahu, HI 96826
(808) 548-4785

This JAPANESE festival begins with a Shinto blessing
ceremony and includes an international trade market,
a queen pageant, a singing contest, a lantern parade,
and demonstrations of the tea ceremony, martial arts,
crafts, calligraphy, ink painting, flower arrangement,
doll making, vegetable carving, paper folding and
cooking. There are also exhibits of antiques,
heirlooms, tray landscapes, bonsai, dolls and carp,
with performances of traditional and modern music.

Dates: mid-Jan-Mar.

* * *

HI164   GIRLS' DAY

Ala Moana Shopping Center, Honolulu, and other stores throughout Hawaii

On JAPANESE Girls' day, dolls of court figures are presented to families with girls, and special doll displays appear in homes and offices. In traditional homes, foods are placed in front of the dolls. Special <u>mochi</u> cakes are sold and paper peach blossoms representing peace in married life are given out in department stores. Holiday dinners are served in homes.

Date: Mar 3.

* * *

HI165   NARCISSUS FESTIVAL

Chinatown, Honolulu, Oahu

Festival Committee
Chinese Chamber of Commerce of Hawaii
42 North King St.
Honolulu, Oahu, HI 96817
(808) 533-3181

The Honolulu CHINESE ethnic community celebrates the Chinese New Year with a round of activities. These include a queen pageant and a coronation ball, the annual Narcissus Flower Show at the Honolulu Academy of Arts, a cooking program, traditional dancing, and a fashion show of modern dress which is usually choreographed on a traditional theme. During the New Year period, there is also open house in Chinatown where merchandise appropriate to the New Year is on display. To the sound of exploding firecrackers, lion dance teams move through the streets, stopping in front of the shops to receive packets of money wrapped in special red envelopes from the businesses' owners. This offering should bring the business prosperity in the year to come. The Narcissus Queen and her court also make a tour of Chinatown, calling on the district's merchants. Movies produced in Hong Kong are presented in local theaters. The New Year's celebration ends with a banquet to which the general public is also welcome.

Dates: Lunar New Year (see dates for coming years in Festivals introduction).

Slides are made of the festival events by the Chinese Chamber of Commerce.

* * *

Hawaii

HI166   SHINTO THANKSGIVING FESTIVAL

        Daijingu Temple, off Pali Highway, Diamond Head

        Daijingu Temple
        61 Puiwa Road
        Honolulu, Oahu, HI 96813

        This traditional JAPANESE harvest festival is held
        to commemorate the ancestors and in Hawaii to bring
        blessings to the state and its officals. A procession
        carrying the spirit on a portable altar out of the
        temple brings good fortune to those near it. A dinner
        is held with Japanese folk dances and marital arts
        demonstrations as entertainment.

        Date: a Sunday in early Oct.

                            * * *

IL167   BON ODORI

        Chicago Midwest Buddhist Temple

        James T. Nishimura
        Midwest Buddhist Temple
        435 W. Menomonee St.
        Chicago, IL 60614
        (312) 943-7801

        An Obon service and dance with traditional JAPANESE
        folk dancing and drumming is held. Paper lanterns
        decorate the dancing area.

        Date: 2nd weekend in July.

        Visitors are invited.

                            * * *

IL168   CHINATOWN SUMMER FAIR AND ART CONTEST

        Cermak and Wentworth Ave., Chicago

        Chicago's Chinatown Chamber of Commerce
        208 W. Cermak Rd.
        Chicago, IL 60616
        (312) 326-5320

        Events at this CHINESE festival include cultural
        dances, martial arts demonstrations, arts and crafts
        demonstrations and sales, food booths, a fashion show,
        both modern and traditional musical performances, and
        a Miss Chinatown pageant. A special event of
        Chicago's festival is the Art Fair Competition, where
        amateur artists of Asian descent display painting,
        handicrafts, sculpture and photography with Asian

IL168   (Chinatown Summer Fair and Art Contest)
cont.
         themes and enter their works in competition with other
         artists.

         Dates: end of July or early Aug.

                              * * *

IL169   GINZA FESTIVAL

         Chicago Midwest Buddhist Temple

         James T. Nishimura
         Midwest Buddhist Temple
         435 W. Menomonee St.
         Chicago, IL 60614
         (312) 943-7801

         JAPANESE cultural exhibits at the Ginza festival
         include a <u>samurai</u> sword display, flower arrangements,
         <u>bonsai</u>, calligraphy and brush painting. Performances
         and demonstrations include classical dancing, folk
         dancing, flower arranging, <u>taiko</u> drumming, and martial
         arts. Japanese food and novelties are sold.

         Date: 3rd weekend in Aug.

         Admission charge.

                              * * *

IL170   KOREAN DAY FESTIVAL

         Lawrence Avenue from E Kedzie, West to Pulaski,
         Chicago

         Korean American Association of Chicago
         5941 N. Ave.
         Chicago, IL 60659
         (312) 878-1900

         Every other year the KOREAN American Association
         sponsors a festival with a parade down Lawrence
         Avenue, art displays, cooking demonstrations, folk
         dances, food booths, a traditional fashion show,
         and live traditional and modern performances.

         Date: early Sept.

                              * * *

MD171   CHINESE LUNAR NEW YEAR FESTIVAL

         Grace and St. Peter's Chinese Ministry
         707 Park Ave., Baltimore

MD171   (Chinese Lunar New Year Festival)
cont.
           Lillian Lee Kim, Director and Coordinator
           524 Anneslie Road
           Baltimore, MD   21212
           (301) 539-1395

           CHINESE New Year is celebrated with a dinner and
           church services, as well as with an art display, folk
           dances, a dragon dance and other traditional events.

           Dates: Lunar New Year (see dates for coming years in
                  Festivals introduction).

           Services held at Park and Monument, entertainment at
           861 Park Ave., dinner and art displays at 707 Park
           Ave. Advance paid reservations needed for dinner.

                                 * * *

MA172   HANAMI

           Arnold Arboretum, Jamaica Plain

           Japan Society of Boston
           22 Batterymarch Street
           Boston, MA 02109

           Viewing of the spring flowers, JAPANESE bonsai and
           flower arrangement displays, as well as other events.

           Date: Mother's Day.

           The Japan Society of Boston, which also sponsors a New
           Year's celebration, maintains an archives of its
           history from 1904-1987.

                                 * * *

MO173   CHINESE CULTURE FESTIVAL

           St. Louis

           Organization of Chinese Americans, St. Louis Chapter
           12077 Lake Placid Dr.
           St. Louis, MO 63146
           (314) 694-6830

           CHINESE arts and crafts displays, traditional dances,
           traditional and modern fashion shows, cooking displays
           and live performances.

           Date: in Sept, every three years.

           Has photographs and slides of previous festivals.

                                 * * *

                               Maryland-Massachusetts-Missouri

MO174 JAPANESE FESTIVAL

Missouri Botanical Garden, St. Louis

Deborah Graham, Events Coordinator
Missouri Botanical Garden
P.O. Box 299
St. Louis, MO 63166
(314) 577-5125

JAPANESE flower and plant displays, flower arranging,
tea ceremony, craft displays, cooking demonstrations,
food sales, traditional Japanese fashion show, live
performances, cultural dances, and Japanese movies.

Date: annually in late Sept, for several days.

Has archival materials, including photographs,
videotapes and other historical materials on past
festivals. These are accessible to researchers by
appointment.

* * *

MO175 V. P. FAIR

St. Louis

Organization of Chinese Americans, St. Louis Chapter
12077 Lake Placid Dr.
St. Louis, MO 63146
(314) 694-6830

The chapter holds a fair with craft displays,
traditional dances and other live traditional and
modern Chinese performances. Chinese food sales.

Date: early July.

Maintains photographs and slides which are accessible
to researchers by appointment.

* * *

NY176 ASIAN AMERICAN FESTIVAL

Columbus Park, Bayard and Mulberry St.
Chinatown, New York

Alan Chow, Executive Director
Chinese American Arts Council
45 Canal St., 2/F
New York, NY 10002
(212) 431-9740

Since 1976, this annual festival has offered
performances of the music and dances of the Asian

NY176   (Asian American Festival)
cont.
        Pacific area. KOREAN, JAPANESE, CHINESE, VIETNAMESE,
        INDONESIAN, PHILIPPINE, and THAI, as well as INDIAN,
        TAHITIAN and HAWAIIAN cultures are represented. The
        dances are traditional, historic, regional and modern
        and are performed mainly by Asian American dance
        companies in the New York area. Japanese <u>karate</u>, Thai
        martial arts and <u>kung-fu</u> are also demonstrated.

        Date: a Sunday in Sept.

                              * * *

NY177   CHINATOWN SUMMER CULTURAL FESTIVAL

        Columbus Park, Bayard and Mulberry St., New York

        Alan Chow, Executive Director
        Chinese American Arts Council
        45 Canal St., 2/F
        New York, NY 10002
        (212) 431-9740

        Now a major annual event in New York's Chinatown, this
        summer festival was instituted in 1971 to promote
        CHINESE traditional culture, provide free community
        entertainment and be a showcase for talented Asian
        American individuals and performing groups. The
        festival performances include traditional, folk and
        modern dances by Chinese Dance Companies, Chinese
        instrumental music, martial arts and <u>tai-chi</u>
        demonstrations, excerpts from Peking and Cantonese
        Opera, as well as live performances by Chinese pop
        and folk singers. Chinese art shows are also offered.

        Dates: weekends in July and Aug.

                              * * *

NY178   CHINESE NEW YEAR

        Chinatown, bounded by Baxter St. on the West, Park Row
        and the Bowery on the South and East and Canal Street
        on the North, New York

        Alan Chow, Executive Director
        Chinese-American Arts Council
        45 Canal St., 2/F
        New York, NY 10002
        (212) 431-9740

        Music, dragon and lion dancers parade in the streets
        of Chinatown to the sound of firecrackers. CHINESE
        folk dances, <u>kung-fu</u> exhibitions and other special
        activities are presented, and special foods are sold.
        The New Year celebration ends on the fifteenth day of

NY178   (Chinese New Year)
cont.
        the first lunar month when, led by dragon dancers,
        children parade through the street with lanterns they
        have made.

        Dates: Lunar New Year (see dates for coming years in
               Festivals introduction).

                              * * *

OH179   CHINESE NEW YEAR'S

        Cleveland State Univ. Campus

        Jackson Tung, Chapter President
        Organization of Chinese Americans, Cleveland Chapter
        113 Sussex
        Hudson, OH 44236

        The CHINESE New Year's celebration held on campus has
        food sales and displays, a traditional fashion show
        and live traditional performances.

        Dates: Lunar New Year (see dates for coming years in
               Festivals introduction).

                              * * *

OR180   KAM WAH CHUNG DAYS

        City Park and other sites in John Day

        Grant County Chamber of Commerce
        710 S. Canyon Blvd.
        John Day, OR 97845
        (503) 575-0547

        A festival to celebrate the history of the CHINESE in
        John Day, a gold mining town with a trading post which
        continued to serve the Chinese community in Eastern
        Oregon into the 1940's. Demonstrations include
        traditional Chinese dances and music, as well as
        crafts and other exhibits. Local flower and art clubs
        participate with a cultural exhibit. A highlight
        of the festival is a traditional Chinese evening
        parade with a Kam Wah Chung Princess, lion dancing,
        rickshaw races, martial arts, and fireworks.

        Dates: two days in Sept.

        Admission charge to festival.

        Cf. KAM WAH CHUNG AND CO. MUSEUM, OR68
            KAM WAH CHUNG COMPANY BUILDING, OR140.

                              * * *

                                         New York-Ohio-Oregon

PA181   CHINESE NEW YEAR CELEBRATION

Univ. of Pennsylvania Museum, Philadelphia

Robert Arbuckle, Assistant, Museum Events
University of Pennsylvania Museum
33rd and Spruce Sts.
Philadelphia, PA 19104
(215) 898-3024

Since 1982, the University Museum has arranged a day-
long cultural program with an emphasis on interactive,
participatory demonstrations of traditional CHINESE
arts, crafts, games and cuisine, and with traditional
performances and films. Some recent programs have
included demonstrations of martial arts, calligraphy,
penjing (tray landscapes), papercutting, knot tying,
Chinese chess, and mahjong as well as Peking Opera
performances. The museum also offers a dim-sum
luncheon and celebrates with a traditional lion dance
and firecracker parade.

Date: a day during the Chinese Lunar New Year period
      (see Lunar New Year dates for coming years in
      Festivals introduction).

No admission charge to museum; donations requested.

* * *

UT182   OBON FESTIVAL

Salt Lake Buddhist Temple, Salt Lake City

Reverend C. Yakumo
Salt Lake Buddhist Temple
211 West First South
Salt Lake City, UT 84101
(801) 363-4742

Holds JAPANESE Buddhist religious services and
organizes traditional Obon Festival folk dancing.
Other cultural events are also held during the
festival period, including an art contest and display
and traditional performances. Traditional Japanese
foods are served at food booths.

Date: early July.

Maintains archival materials in the temple library,
including photographs and videotapes on past
festivals. Visitors are welcome to participate in
some activities.

* * *

WA183   CHINATOWN INTERNATIONAL DISTRICT SUMMER FESTIVAL

South King St. and Maynard Ave.,
Hing Hay Park, Seattle

Chinatown Chamber of Commerce
508 1/2 7th Ave. South
Seattle, WA 98104
(206) 623-8179

Asian American communities from the greater Seattle
area participate in this festival which includes a
street parade and various activities in Hing Hay Park.
Festivals feature such entertainment as THAI and
FILIPINO folk dancers, Asian American jazz bands,
martial arts experts, CHINESE drill teams, JAPANESE
taiko drummers, and demonstrations in a special
Learning World where children are taught folk arts
and crafts. These may include origami, face painting,
and wind sock making, as well as puppetry. HMONG
needlework and Chinese herbs are also displayed.
Food booths offer traditional foods.

Dates: mid-July.

Maintains photographs, videotapes, and other
historical materials on past festival celebrations
and ethnic history. These materials are accessible to
researchers by appointment.

* * *

WA184   CHINATOWN QUEEN PAGEANT

Chinatown, 7th and Maynard, Seattle

Chinatown Chamber of Commerce
508 1/2 7th Ave. South
Seattle, WA 98104
(206) 623-8179

In coordination with the National Ms. Chinatown USA
Pageant in San Francisco, the Seattle chapter of the
Chinese Chamber of Commerce holds its own pageant to
select a candidate. The pageant includes CHINESE
dance, fashion shows, and live performances.

Date: mid-Oct.

Maintains photographs, videotapes and other historical
materials accessible to reseachers.

* * *

WA185   CHINESE NEW YEAR FESTIVAL

Chinatown, 7th and Maynard, Seattle

Chinatown Chamber of Commerce
508 1/2 7th St. South
Seattle, WA 98104
(206) 623-8179

CHINESE New Year is celebrated with a parade and lion
dances, a craft display, cooking demonstrations, food
sales and live performances of traditional, as well as
modern music.

Dates: Lunar New Year (see dates for coming years in
       Festivals introduction).

Maintains archival materials accessible to
researchers.

                        * * *

WA186   SOUTHEAST ASIAN FESTIVAL

Southeast Asian Center House, Seattle

Alean Orki
Southeast Asian Refugee Federation Office
2200 Ranier Avenue South
Seattle, WA 98144
(206) 625-2459 or 323-9365

The festival performances include CAMBODIAN dances,
VIETNAMESE music, LAOTIAN dance, and ethnic CHINESE
costume shows; arts and crafts and flower and plant
displays, fashion shows, and other cultural events
from the rich cultural heritage of Seattle's
Southeast Asian community are also a part of the
celebration.

Date: contact Southeast Asian Refugee Federation
Office

Archival materials are available from the Refugee
Federation Office.

                        * * *

WI187   HOLIDAY FOLK FAIR

Mecca, 500 W. Kilbourn Ave., Milwaukee

International Institute of Wisconsin
2810 West Highland Boulevard
Milwaukee, WI 53208
(414) 933-0521

WI187   (Holiday Folk Fair)
cont.
        A 43 year old festival with cultural exhibits, live
        folk music and dance performances, handicrafts and
        food booths representing 36 ethnic groups, including
        the following Asian Americans: CHINESE, JAPANESE,
        KOREAN, FILIPINO, and VIETNAMESE. Each year, special
        recognition is given to one ethnic group. The main
        sponsor is the International Institute, an
        organization whose purpose is to "help immigrants and
        refugees to adapt to American culture and ethnic
        groups to celebrate their rich and diverse heritage."

        Dates: the weekend before Thanksgiving.

                            * * *

WI188   CHINESE NEW YEAR

        Milwaukee businesses, Milwaukee Public Museum, and
        other selected locations.

        Daniel Chen, President.
        Organization of Chinese Americans, Wisconsin Chapter
        6906 Tacoma St.
        Milwaukee, WI 53224

        Dr. Lou Tiu, President
        Chinese-American Civic Club of Milwaukee
        12226 Verona Ct.
        West Allis, WI 53227

        In the past 20 years the number of people of CHINESE
        descent living in Milwaukee has been increasing
        greatly. Now over 3000 Chinese live in the Greater
        Milwaukee area. At Lunar New Year's there are many
        special events; the Chinese American Civic Club
        sponsors programs with demonstrations of painting,
        calligraphy, papercutting, kung-fu, food preparation
        and games, as well as with folk song and dance
        performances, fashion shows, films and Chinese
        American photographic displays.

        Date: Lunar New Year (see dates for coming years in
              Festivals introduction).

                            * * *

BC189   ASIAN PACIFIC FESTIVAL

        Vancouver

        Vancouver Travel Infocenter
        562 Burrard St.
        Vancouver, BC V6C 2J6
        (604) 683-2000

BC189   (Asian Pacific Festival)
cont.
        A festival in which all Asian Pacific cultures in
        Vancouver participate. Features folk dance
        performances and arts and crafts displays. Ends with
        the city's Canada Day celebrations of July 1.

        Dates: late June-July 1.

                              * * *

ON190   JAPANESE FESTIVAL

        Harbourfront

        Japan Canada Society
        235 Queen's Quay West
        Toronto, ON M5S 2C3
        (416) 364-5665

        This JAPANESE festival features craft displays,
        including bonsai and ikebana, calligraphy, poetry,
        martial arts, and fashion shows of traditional dress.

        Dates: early June, 3 days.

                              * * *

QE191   JAPANESE CANADIAN CULTURAL EVENTS

        Cultural Centre and Buddhist Church

        Kathleen Hayami, President
        Japanese Canadian Cultural Centre
        8155 Rousselot St.
        Montreal, Quebec H2E127
        (514) 728-1996, 728-5580

        The cultural centre sponsors activities demonstrating
        JAPANESE traditional arts, such as cooking, ikebana,
        taiko drumming, tea ceremony, go playing, and martial
        arts and offers traditional foods at Quebec Buddhist
        Church Festivals.

        Dates: Apr 26, mid-May, Aug 15, Sept 28 and Nov 10.

        Maintains photographs and historical materials on past
        traditional events and ethnic history.

                              * * *

A Selected List of Material Culture Museums in East and Southeast Asia

The list below includes museums displaying folk arts and crafts and other ethnographical material in the East and Southeast Asian countries from which immigrants have come to North America.

Burma

National Museum of Art and Archaeology
Jubilee Hall, Pagoda Road, Rangoon

China, People's Republic of

Fuzhou Provincial Museum
West Lake, Fuzhou

Guangzhou Museum
Zhen Hai Lou, Yue Xiu Park, Guangzhou

Hubei Provincial Museum
East Park, Wuchang, Wuhan

Jiangsu Provincial Museum
321 E. Zhong Shan Nan Lu, Nanjing

Minorities Cultural Palace Museum
Chang An Boulevard West, Beijing

Shanghai Art and History Museum
Nanjing East Road, Shanghai

Suzhou Historical Museum
Xi Bei Street, Suzhou

China, People's Republic of
cont.
        Tianjin Art Museum
        77 Jie Fang Bei, Tianjin

        Tianjin History Museum
        335 Machang Road, Tianjin

        Wuhan Arts and Crafts Building
        Zhongshan Dadao Road, Hankou, Wuhan

        Zhejiang Provincial Museum
        Wen Lan Ge Buildings, Hangzhou

China, Republic of (Taiwan)

        Formosan Aboriginal Culture Village
        45 Chintien Lane, Talin Village, Yuchih Hsiang
        Nantou County

        Institute of Ethnology, Academia Sinica
        Nankang, Taipei

        Lu-kang Folk Material Culture Museum
        Lu-kang

        Taichung City Cultural Center and Museum of
        Material Culture, 600 Ying-tsai Road, Taichung

        Tainan County Museum of History and Material Culture
        Cheng Ta University, Tainan

        Tainan Municipal Material Culture Museum
        152 Kai-Shan Road, Tainan

        Tainan Municipal Yung-Han Folk Art Museum
        43 Kuo-Sheng Road, Anping District, Tainan

        Taiwan Folk Art and Antique House
        32 Yu-Ya Road, Peitou

        Taiwan Provincial Museum
        #2 Siangyang Road, Taipei

Hong Kong

        Hong Kong Museum of History
        Blocks S61 and S62, Kowloon Park, Haiphong Road
        Tsimshatsui, Kowloon

Indonesia

        Anthropological Museum
        Cendrawasih University, Abepura, Irian Jaya

        Bali Museum
        Denpasar, Bali

Indonesia
cont.

Museum Indonesia
Taman Mini, Jakarta (South)

National Museum
Medan Merdeka West, Barat 12, Jakarta

Ujung Pandang Provincial Museum
Amsterdam Castle, Ujung Pandang, Sulawesi (The
Celebes)

Wayang Museum Fatahillah Square West
Old Batavia, Jakarta

Japan

Chido Museum
10-18 Kachu-shinmachi, Tsuruoka-shi, Yamagata-ken

Edo Village
He-19, Yuwaku-machi, Kanazawa-shi, Ishikawa-ken

Hida Folklore Village and Museum
Kamiokamoto-cho, Takayama-shi, Gifu-ken

International Christian University
Hachiro Yuasa Memorial Museum
10-2, Osawa 3-chome, Mitaka-shi, Tokyo

Iwate Prefectural Museum
34 Ueda Aza Matsuyashiki, Morioka-shi, Iwate-ken

Japan Folk Art Museum
7-6 Nambanaka 3-chome, Naniwa-ku, Osaka

Japan Folk Art Museum, Okinawa Branch,
1-30 Kinjo-cho, Shuri, Naha-shi, Okinawa-ken

Japan Folk Crafts Museum
4-3-33 Komaba, Meguro-ku, Tokyo

Japan Folk Crafts Museum
10-5 Banpaku Koen, Senri, Suita-shi, Osaka

Japan Folklore Museum
4-1 Marunouchi, Matsumoto-shi, Nagano-ken

Kanagawa Prefectural Museum
5-60 Minaminaka-dori, Naka-ku, Yokohama-shi
Kanagawa-ken

Kumamoto International Folk Art Museum
Sannomiya Koen, 593 Kami-Tatsuta, Tatsuta-machi
Kumamoto-shi, Kumamoto-ken

Kurashiki Museum of Folk Crafts
1-4-11 Chuo, Kurashiki-shi, Okayama-ken

Japan
cont.
        Kyoto Prefectural Exhibition Hall
        Nakaragi-cho, Shimogamo, Sakyo-ku, Kyoto

        Matsumoto Folk Arts Museum
        1313-1 Shimoganai, Satoyamabe, Matsumoto-shi
        Nagano-ken

        Morioka City Local History Hall
        14-1 Atago-cho, Morioka-shi, Iwate-ken

        Okinawa Prefectural Museum
        1-1 Onaka-machi, Shuri, Naha-shi, Okinawa-ken

        Old Tamba Pottery Museum
        185 Kawara-machi, Sasayama-cho, Taki-gun, Hyogo-ken

        Open-Air Museum of Old Japanese Farmhouses
        1-2 Hattori Ryokuchi, Toyonaka-shi, Osaka

        Osaka City Museum
        1-1 Osaka-jo, Higashi-ku, Osaka-shi

        Saitama Prefectural Historical Museum
        757 Oaza Sugaya, Ranzan-cho, Hiki-gun, Saitama-ken

        Seto City History and Folklore Gallery
        1 Higashi Matsuyama-cho, Seto-shi, Aichi-ken

        Takayama Museum of Local History
        75 Kamiichinomachi, Takayama-shi, Gifu-ken

        Tenri University Sankokan Museum
        1 Furu-machi, Tenri-shi, Nara-ken

        Toyama City Folk Art Village
        1118-1 Anyobo, Toyama-shi, Toyama-ken

Korea, Democratic People's Republic of

        State Central Ethnographic Museum
        Pyongyang

Korea, Republic of

        Cheju Folklore Museum
        Cheju Island

        Museum of Korean Folklore
        Kyong-Bok Palace, Seoul

        University Museum
        Seoul National University, Seoul

        Korean Folk Village
        Yong'in Gun

Philippines

Alto Doll Museum
400 Guevarra Avenue, San Juan, Metro Manila

Bayanihan Folk Arts Center
Philippine Womens University
Taft Avenue, Metro Manila 2801

Kailokuan Historical Ilocano Museum
Vigan House, Nayong Pilipino, Pasay City, 31

Museo Ng Buhay Pilipino
784 Quirino Avenue, Paranaque, Metro Manila 3128

Museum of Anthropology, College of Arts and Sciences
Univ. of the Philippines, Diliman, Quezon City 3004

Museum of Philippine Costumes
Mercury Bldg., T. M. Kalaw Street, Ermita
Metro Manila

Museum of Philippine Traditional Culture
Nayong Pilipino, M.I.A, Pasay City

Silliman University Anthropological Museum
Dumaguete City, 6501

St. Theresa's College Museum
St. Theresa's College, Elizabeth Pond St., Cebu City

Xavier Folklife Museum and Archives
Xavier University, Cagayan de Oro City, 8401

Singapore

National Museum
Stanford Road, Singapore 6

University of Singapore Art Museum and Exhibition
Gallery
University of Singapore, Singapore 10

Thailand

Farmer's Museum and Phiman Mongkut Pavilion
Narai Raja Niwes, Lop Buri

Kamthieng House Museum, Siam Society
131 Asoke Road, Lane 21, Bangkok

National Museum
Naphrathatu Road, Bangkok

Glossary

The transliterations of foreign terms into the phonetic alphabet follow the information provided by collections and organizations listed in this book. Alternative spellings are in parentheses.

batik:
  Javanese method of printing colored designs on cotton or silk by waxing parts not to be dyed

bonsai:
  Japanese art of trimming plant or tree cuttings to create a miniature

dim-sum (dimsum):
  Cantonese style of eating many snack dishes prepared in a variety of ways

go:
  Japanese game played by two persons with black and white stones placed on intersecting lines of a board; opponents capture each other's stones trying to occupy the board

ikebana:
  Japanese flower arrangement made and displayed according to strict rules

Issei (Isei):
  the first generation of Japanese emigrants

kimono:
  Japanese wrap-around robe with wide sleeves and a broad sash worn by men and women

koto:
  Japanese 13-stringed zither; related to Chinese cheng

kung-fu (kungfu; gungfu):
  Chinese art of physical defense following a strict code of behavior and not using weapons

mah-jong (mahjong):
  Chinese game played by four persons with tiles marked in
  sets; tiles are drawn and discarded until one player
  acquires a winning combination

mingei:
  Japanese term for folk art; also may refer to imitation
  of folk art forms and techniques by artist-craftsmen

mochi cakes:
  Japanese sweet cakes made of sticky rice and sometimes
  decorated for special ocassions

mooncakes:
  Chinese round cakes with moulded designs and various kinds
  of fillings; eaten for the Moon Festival on the 15th of the
  8th month by the lunar calendar

netsuki:
  carved toggle formerly used by Japanese men to attach a
  tobacco pouch to the sash of a kimono

Nissei (Nisei):
  the generation born to the first generation of Japanese
  immigrants

origami:
  Japanese art of folding paper into intricate forms

penjing (pen-ching; benjing):
  Chinese art of creating a miniature landscape, usually
  mountainous, out of rocks and plants in a tray

shakuhachi:
  Japanese five-hole flute blown at one end

shamisen:
  Japanese three-stringed plucked lute used to accompany
  folksong and theatrical performances; of Chinese origin

shoji:
  Japanese translucent room partitions which slide to provide
  passage between rooms

taiko:
  large two-headed Japanese barrel drums played with sticks
  on one head; a style of folk drumming for special occasions

ti-chin (t'i-ch'in):
  Chinese bowed two-stringed lute of Mongol origin

tong:
  Cantonese word referring to a secret society of men
  sharing allegiances and commitments

torii:
  Japanese Shinto shrine gateway with two cylindrical posts
  connected by two cross-beams

Bibliography

Immigration History and Asian American Experience

Bulosan, Carlos. America Is in the Heart: A Personal History. Seattle: U of Washington P, 1973. (Reprint of New York: Harcourt, 1943.)

Chan, Anthony B. Gold Mountain: The Chinese in the New World. Vancouver, BC: New Star Books, 1983.

Char, Tin-Yuke, and Wai Jane Char, comp. and ed. Chinese Historic Sites and Pioneer Families of the Island of Hawaii. Honolulu: U of Hawaii P, 1983.

Chinese in America. Amerasia Journal 8:1 (1981). Special Topic Volume.

Con, Harry, Ronald J. Con, Graham Johnson, Edgar Wickberg, and William E. Willmott. From China to Canada: A History of the Chinese Communities in Canada. Toronto: McClelland & Stewart, 1982.

Cordova, Fred. Filipinos: Forgotten Asian Americans. A Pictorial Essay/1763-Circa 1963. Des Moines, IA: Kendall Hunt, 1983.

A Dream of Riches: The Japanese Canadians, 1877-1977. Toronto: Gilchrist Wright, Printer, for Japanese Canadian Centennial Project Committee, Vancouver and Dreadnaught, Toronto, 1978.

Hendricks, Glenn L., Bruce T. Downing, and Amos S. Deinard. The Hmong in Transition. Staten Island, NY: Center for Immigration Studies, 1986.

Hurh, Won Moo, and Kwang Chung Kim. Korean Immigrants
in America: A Structural Analysis of Ethnic Confinement and
Adhesive Adaptation. Rutherford, NJ: Fairleigh Dickinson U
P, 1984.

Kingston, Maxine Hong. China Men. New York: Knopf,
1981.

Kwong, Peter. Chinatown, N.Y.: Labor and Politics,
1930-1950. New York: Monthly Review Press, 1979.

Lee, Rose Hum. The Chinese in the United States of
America. Hong Kong: Hong Kong U P, 1960.

Nakane, Kazuko. Nothing Left in My Hands. Seattle:
Young Pine Press, 1985.

Lukes, Timothy J., and Gary Y. Okihiro. Japanese
Legacy: Farming and Community Life in California's Santa
Clara Valley. Cupertino, CA: California History Center, De
Anza College. (Local History Studies, Vol. 31.)

McDermott, John F., Jr., Wen-Shing Tseng, and Thomas
W. Maretzki. Asians in Hawaii. Honolulu: John A. Burns
School of Medicine and U of Hawaii P, 1980.

Mark, Diane Mei Lin and Ginger Chih. A Place Called
Chinese America. Dubuque, IA: Kendall Hunt for The
Organization of Chinese Americans, 1982.

Meyer, Dillon S. Uprooted Americans: The Japanese
Americans and the War Relocation Authority during World War
II. Tucson: U of Arizona P, 1971.

Miller, Stuart Creighton. The Unwelcome Immigrant:
The American Image of the Chinese, 1785-1882. Berkeley: U of
California P, 1969.

Montero, Darrel. Vietnamese Americans: Patterns of
Resettlement and Socioeconomic Adaptation in the United
States. Boulder, CO: Westview Press, 1979.

Mori, Toshio. Yokohama, California. Seattle: U of
Washington P, 1985. (Reprint of Caxton, ID: Caxton Printers,
1949.

Nee, Victor G., and Brett de Bary. Longtime
Californ': A Documentary Study of an American Chinatown.
Boston: Houghton, 1972.

Ogawa, Dennis M. Jan Ken Po. The World of Hawaii's
Japanese Americans. Honolulu: U of Hawaii P, 1973.

Okada, John. No-No Boy. Seattle: U of Washington P,
1957.

Pido, Antonio, J. A. The Pilipinos in America:
Macro/Micro Dimensions of Immigration and Integration. New
York: Center for Migration Studies, 1985.

Quan, Robert Seto. Lotus among the Magnolias.
Jackson: UP of Mississippi, 1982.

Sandmeyer, Elmer Clarence. The Anti-Chinese Movement
in California. Urbana: U of Illinois P, 1973.

Siu, Paul C. P. The Chinese Laundryman: A Study of
Social Isolation. New York: New York UP, 1987.

Sunahara, Ann Gomer. The Politics of Racism: The
Uprooting of Japanese Canadians during the Second World War.
Toronto: James Lorimer, 1981.

Takaki, Ronald. Pau Hana: Plantation Life and Labor
in Hawaii, 1835-1920. Honolulu: U of Hawaii P, 1983.

Ujimoto, K. Victor, and Gordon Harabayashi. Visible
Minorities and Multiculturism: Asians in Canada. Toronto:
Butterworth, 1980.

Vallangca, Caridad C. The Second Wave: Pinay and
Pinoy. Los Angeles: Philippine Expressions, 1987.

Weglyn, Michi. Years of Infamy: The Untold Story of
America's Concentration Camps. New York: Morrow, 1976.

Young, Charles H., and Helen R. Y. Reid. The Japanese
Canadians. New York: Arno Press, 1978. (Reprint of Toronto:
U of Toronto P, 1938.)

Yung, Judy. Chinese Women of America: A Pictorial
History. Seattle: U of Washington P and the Chinese Culture
Foundation of San Francisco, 1986.

Material Culture and Festival Arts

Aluit, Alfonso J. The Galleon Guide to Philippine
Festivals and Traditional Events. Manila: Galleon, 1969.

Amaury, Saint-Gilles. Mingei: Japan's Enduring Folk
Arts. Tokyo: Heian International, 1983.

Araki, Nancy K., and Jane Horii. Matsuri Festival:
Japanese American Celebrations and Activities. Tokyo: Heian
International, 1978.

Casal, U. A. The Five Sacred Festivals of Ancient
Japan: Their Symbolism and Historical Development. Tokyo:
Sophia U, in cooperation with Charles E. Tuttle, 1967.

Chang, Toy Len. Chinese Festivals the Hawaiian Way.
Honolulu: Toy Len Chang, 1983.

Choe Sang-su. Annual Customs of Korea: Notes on the
Rites and Ceremonies of the Year. Seoul: Korea Book for the
Gyeonggi College Folklore Research Center, 1960.

Chow, Alan. Arts of Chinatown New York. New York:
Chinese-American Arts Council, 1982.

DeFrancis, John. Things Japanese in Hawaii.
Honolulu: U of Hawaii P, 1973.

Ecke, Tseng Yu-ho. Chinese Folk Art II in American
Collections, From Early 15th Century to Early 20th Century.
Honolulu: Tseng Yu-ho Ecke, 1977.

di Franco, Toni L. Chinese Clothing and Theatrical
Costumes in the San Joaquin County Historical Museum. Lodi,
CA: San Joaquin County Historical Museum, 1981.

Gittinger, Mattiebelle. Splendid Symbols: Textiles
and Tradition in Indonesia. Washington, DC: The Textile
Museum, 1979.

Haga, Hideo. Japanese Folk Festivals, Illustrated.
Trans. Fanny Hagin Mayer. Tokyo: Miura Printing, 1970.

Hauge, Victor and Takako. Folk Traditions in Japanese
Art. Tokyo: Kodansha International, 1978.

Kahlenberg, Mary Hung. Textile Traditions of
Indonesia. Los Angeles, CA: Los Angeles County Museum of
Art, 1977.

Kates, George. N. Chinese Household Furniture. New
York: Dover, 1948.

Malm, William P. Music Cultures of the Pacific, the
Near East, and Asia 2d ed. Englewood Cliffs, NJ: Prentice,
1977.

Moes, Robert. Mingei: Japanese Folk Art from the
Brooklyn Museum Collection. New York: Universe Books, 1985.

Muraoka, Kageo, and Kichiemon Okamura. Folk Arts and
Crafts of Japan. Trans. Daphne D. Stegmaier. New York and
Tokyo: Weatherhill/Heibonsha, 1973. (Vol. 26 of the Heibonsha
Survey of Japanese Art.)

Rathbun, William J., and Michael Knight. Yo no Bi:
The Beauty of Japanese Folk Art. Seattle: Seattle Art, 1983.

Stalberg, Roberta Helmer, and Ruth Nesi. China's
Crafts. New York: Eurasia Press, 1980.

Wells, Mariann K. "Chinese Temples in California."
MA Thesis, U of California at Berkeley, 1962.

Yanagi, Soetsu. The Unknown Craftsman: A Japanese
Insight into Beauty. Adapted by Bernard Leach. Tokyo:
Kodansha International, 1972.

Reference Works

American Buddhist Directory. New York: American
Buddhist Movement, 1985.

Caberoy, Francisca F. Directory of Museums in the
Philippines. Manila: National Museum, 1984.

California Historical Landmarks. Sacramento:
California Dept. of Parks and Recreation, 1979, rev. 1982.

Char, Tin-Yuke, and Wai Jane Char, comp. and ed.
Chinese Historic Sites and Pioneer Families of the Island of
Hawaii. Honolulu: U of Hawaii P, 1983.

Directory of Canadian Museums and Related
Institutions, 1984-85. Ottawa: Canadian Museums Assoc.,
1984-85.

Folklife Sourcebook. Washington, DC: American
Folklife Center, Library of Congress, 1986.

Gregory, Ruth W. Anniversaries and Holidays. 3d ed.
Chicago: American Library Association, 1975.

Hawaii Cultural Resource Directory, 1983. Honolulu:
State Foundation on Culture and the Arts, 1983.

Hudson, Kenneth, and Ann Nicholls. The Directory of
Museums and Living Displays. 3d ed. Henley, England:
Macmillan, 1985.

Kim, Hong N. Scholars' Guide to Washington, D.C. for
East Asian Studies. Washington, DC: Smithsonian Institution
Press, 1979. (Woodrow Wilson International Center for
Scholars.)

Kitano, Harry H. L., comp. Asians in America: A
Selected Bibliography for Use in Social Work Education. New
York: Council on Social Work Education, 1971.

Kornrich, Bill, ed. Calendar of Festivals.
Washington, DC: National Council for the Traditional Arts,
1980.

Lai, Him Mark. A History Reclaimed: An Annotated
Bibliography of Chinese Language Materials on the Chinese of
America. English Language Edition ed. Russell Leong and Jean
Pang Yip. Los Angeles: Asian American Studies Center, UCLA,
1986.

Liu, John M. "1982 Selected Bibliography." Amerasia
9:2 (1982), 147-172.

National Register of Historic Places, 1976. 2 vols.
Washington, DC: U.S. Department of the Interior, 1976.

The Official Museum Directory, 1986. Washington, DC:
American Association of Museums, 1986.

Ong, Paul M. and William Wong Lum. Theses and
Dissertations on Asians in the United States. Davis: U of
California Asian American Studies, Dept. of Applied
Behavioral Sciences, September 1974.

Roberts, Laurance P. Roberts' Guide to Japanese
Museums of Art and Archaeology. Tokyo: Simul Press, 1987.

Shemenski, Frances. A Guide to World Fairs and
Festivals. Westport, CT: Greenwood, 1985.

Smith, Betty Pease, comp. and ed. Directory of
Historical Agencies in North America. 13th ed. Nashville,
TN: American Assoc. for State and Local History, 1986.

Thernstrom, Stephan, ed. Harvard Encyclopedia of
American Ethnic Groups. Cambridge, MA: Harvard UP, 1980.

Wasserman, Paul, and Edmond L. Applebaum, eds.
Festivals Sourcebook. 2d ed. Detroit: Gale Research, 1984.

Wasserman, Paul, and Jean Morgan, eds. Ethnic
Information Sources of the United States. Detroit: Gale
Research, 1976.

Wei Chi Poon. Directory of Asian American Collections
in the United States. Berkeley: U of California, Asian
American Studies Library, 1982.

Wynar, Lubomyr R., and Anna T. Encyclopedic Directory
of Ethnic Newspapers and Periodicals in the United States.
2d ed. Littleton, CO: Libraries Unlimited, 1976.

Wynar, Lubomyr R., and Lois Buttla, eds. Guide to
Ethnic Museums, Libraries, and Archives in the United States.
Kent, OH: Kent State U, Center for Ethnic Publications, 1978.

Young, Judith. Celebrations: America's Best
Festivals, Jamborees, Carnivals and Parades. Santa Barbara,
CA: Capra Press, 1986.

Name Index

General Index

The terms used in this index belong to the following categories: objects of material culture; major sources for historical study, such as photographic, video and film collections; significant events, persons and places in Asian American history; and annual celebrations. These terms are further subdivided into subentries according to ethnic group when this information is available and relevant. When specific information about the cultural origin of an item is unavailable, the term "Asian" or "Asian American" is used.

The entries for collections (AZ1-ON103), historical sites (AR104-BC144), and festivals (AZ145-QE191) are arranged in numerical order. The user may determine the geographical location, the state or province, of a collection, site or festival by referring to the letter codes prefixed to each entry number. These letter codes may be ignored, however, when the user is trying to find an entry cited in the index. The letter codes are explained on the following page.

EXPLANATION OF LETTER CODES

UNITED STATES		United States (cont.)	
Arizona	AZ	Texas	TX
Arkansas	AR	Utah	UT
California	CA	Virginia	VA
Colorado	CO	Washington	WA
Connecticut	CT	Wisconsin	WI
District of Columbia	DC	Wyoming	WY
Florida	FL		
Hawaii	HI	CANADA	
Idaho	ID	British Columbia	BC
Illinois	IL	Manitoba	MB
Indiana	IN	Ontario	ON
Iowa	IA	Quebec	QE
Kansas	KS		
Maryland	MD		
Massachusetts	MA		
Michigan	MI		
Minnesota	MN		
Missouri	MO		
Montana	MT		
New Hampshire	NH		
New Jersey	NJ		
New Mexico	NM		
New York	NY		
Ohio	OH		
Oregon	OR		
Pennsylvania	PA		
Tennessee	TN		

Tobacco, OR68

Tomokiyo, Seichi, Carpenter,
    HI136

Tong (Tung):
  Sam Yap, CA108
  Yan Woo, CA108
  War of 1854, CA127
  Tong Wo, HI129

Tools:
  Ainu, NY61
  Burmese, IA49
  Chinese, CA4, CA5, CA8,
      CA12, CA13, CA20, CA25,
      DC32, HI35, ID43, ID44,
      IA49, NM60, WI79, WY82,
      BC83, BC84, BC94, BC98
  Indonesian, MO55, NM60
  Japanese, CA17, FL34, HI36,
      HI40, IA49, MO55, NH58,
      NM60, TX73, WI79, BC88,
      BC98
  Korean, CA17, MO55
  Laotian, DC32
  Malay, MO55
  Philippine, CA17, HI36,
      MO55, NH58, TX73, VA74,
      WA76
  Thai, MO55, NH58, NM60
  Vietnamese, IL45, MO55,
      WA76

Tope, Joseph C., Collector,
    CA8

Torii gates, Japanese, CA117,
    HI136, HI137

Toys:
  Burmese, NM60
  Chinese, CA13, CA14, CA17,
      CA20, CT30, ID43, IA49,
      MO55, PA70, TX72, TX73,
      VA74, WI79, BC92, BC94,
      BC98
  Indonesian, CA14, MO55,
      NM60
  Japanese, CA8, CA10, CA14,
      CA17, CA23, CT30, FL34,
      HI40, HI42, IA49, MA52,
      MI53, MN54, MO55, NM60,
      NY61, PA70, TX72, TX73,
      WI79, BC87, BC98
  Javan, CT30
  Korean, CA14, MO56, NM60,
      WI79
  Malay, MO55

Toys (cont.):
  Philippine, CA14, CA17,
      TX73, WA76
  Thai, MO55, NM60
  Vietnamese, MO55

Trading post, Chinese,
    OR68, OR140

Transcontinental railroad.
    See Canadian Pacific
    Railroad; Central
    Pacific Railroad

Transport:
  Chinese, CA13, IA49, TX72
  Japanese, IA49, NH58

Trees:
  Chinese, CA123
  Japanese, CA112
  See also Bonsai; Penjing

Tunnels. See Constructions

Umbrellas, Japanese, PA70

Utah Festival, UT182

Vases:
  Chinese, CA13, NY62
  Japanese, IA49
  See also Ceramics

Videotapes:
  Asian American, HI41, OR69,
      NY64
  Burmese, DC154
  Chinese, OR69, BC100,
      WA183, WA184,
  Japanese, BC100, MO174,
      UT182

Vietnamese:
  Collections, CA12, CA15,
      CA17, CA18, DC33, HI40,
      ID43, IL45, MA50, MN54,
      MO55, NY61, OR67, TX73,
      WA76, WI79, BC98, ON103
  Festivals, DC155, NY176,
      WA186, WI187

Virginia Collections, VA74-
    VA75

Wagner, Mrs. C. Madeline,
    Collector, CA6

Wah Hop, Settler, CA4